STOP Yelling, START Connecting WITH Your Child

Peaceful Parenting Guide to Handle Misbehavior, Tame Tantrums, and Raise Emotionally Resilient Kids

Carrie Khang

© Copyright Carrie Khang 2025 - All rights reserved.

The content contained within this book may not be reproduced, duplicated, or transmitted without direct written permission from the author or the publisher.

Under no circumstances will any blame or legal responsibility be held against the publisher, or author, for any damages, reparation, or monetary loss due to the information contained within this book. Either directly or indirectly. You are responsible for your own choices, actions, and results.

Legal Notice:

This book is copyright protected. This book is only for personal use. You cannot amend, distribute, sell, use, quote, or paraphrase any part, or the content within this book, without the consent of the author or publisher.

Disclaimer Notice:

Please note the information contained within this document is for educational and entertainment purposes only. All effort has been executed to present accurate, up to date, and reliable, complete information. No warranties of any kind are declared or implied. Readers acknowledge that the author is not engaging in the rendering of legal, financial, medical, or professional advice. The content within this book has been derived from various sources. Please consult a licensed professional before attempting any techniques outlined in this book.

By reading this document, the reader agrees that under no circumstances is the author responsible for any losses, direct or indirect, which are incurred as a result of the use of the information contained within this document, including, but not limited to, — errors, omissions, or inaccuracies.

Before You Begin, grab your gift!

Because parenting is hard, and you're doing the work. I've put together a collection of practical tools to support you beyond this book.

🎁 From calming strategies to printable activities for your kids, these bonus resources are yours, completely free!

👉 Scan the QR code

📦 Includes:
- ✔ *Top 10 Yelling Triggers*
- ✔ *7-Day Self-Care for Moms*
- ✔ *5-Minute Gratitude Journal for Kids*
- ✔ *How do I? Printable Worksheet*
- ✔ *The Gratitude Journal for Moms*

https://carriekhang.com

Other Books by Carrie Khang:

CONTENTS

Introduction 7
Part I: Understanding Your Anger
    Chapter 1: Why You Really Yell 11
    Chapter 2: The Anger Underneath 25
    Chapter 3: Know Your Parenting Style 37
Part II: Stay Calm, Take Control
    Chapter 4: The Calm Starts With You 49
    Chapter 5: Say It Better 63
    Chapter 6: Why Self-Care 79
Part III: Understanding Your Child
    Chapter 7: What's Behind Your Child's Behavior? 95
    Chapter 8: Real Strategies For Real Challenges 111
    Chapter 9: Magical Consequences 129
Part IV: Building Connection
    Chapter 10: Connection B4 Correction 143
    Chapter 11: When You And Your Partner Clash 157
    Chapter 12: Be The Parent You Want To Be 169
Conclusion 181
Bonus: Frequently Asked Questions 185
Reference And Further Reading 191

INTRODUCTION

"Children are not a distraction from more important work. They are the most important work." – C.S. Lewis

This book isn't written from a perfect place. It is written by someone who has experienced frustration, guilt, and a deep desire to improve, and who has also studied what helps.

If you have a child between the ages of 3 and 10 years and are striving to raise them with love, compassion, and empathy rather than with anger, then this book is for you. I wrote it to provide a guiding light for when parenting feels overwhelming, offering actionable tools to strengthen your relationship with your child and your partner.

Have you ever found yourself gazing at your child as they sleep, your heart heavy with regret for the times your voice rose too high? Perhaps you've gently stroked their cheek, promising silently to do better, longing for those "movie moments," where parent and child are always laughing, always happy.

"I swear I'll never yell," you might tell yourself.

Yet here you are, loving your child more than anything, wondering, "Why can't I stay calm?" You aren't alone. Admitting that you want to lead with love instead of anger isn't a sign of failure, but a testament to your desire to be a better parent. Behind every raised voice is a deeper story waiting to be understood. In this book, you'll learn that being a parent is about being present, not perfect.

This book *won't* teach you how to get it all "right," but it *will* teach you to discover the meaning behind your actions and your children's reactions.

Part 1 will help you identify the root of your anger and determine its source. Part 2 will provide you with the tools to help you stay calm during tough situations and respond more effectively to your child's needs. Parts 3 and 4 will help you to better understand your child and build stronger connections.

When you see a pencil ✏ icon, that's your cue to grab something to write with and get ready for a thought exercise. You'll also see a section named **"Parent Perspectives"** sprinkled throughout the book, which provides real-life scenarios and perspectives from parents who have faced many of the parenting challenges that you might be facing now.

This book isn't a textbook on anger, but rather a valuable resource to help you navigate parenthood from a place of love and empathy, rather than anger. This is the space where you lose it over spilled juice, where bedtime becomes a battlefield, where you question yourself if you're doing anything right. Please rest assured that you are.

Just by seeking out this book, you're taking a step towards curiosity and compassion. You're choosing to show up, even when the days feel impossibly hard. It's about one breath, one pause, one meaningful repair—a gentle reminder that change isn't an overhaul; it's a series of small, intentional steps.

You're here because you care. You've already begun the journey of parenthood—welcome to the next adventure.

Understanding Your Anger

Part 1

CHAPTER 1

WHY YOU REALLY YELL

"Behind every child who acts out is an unmet need or an emotion they can't name." – L.R. Knost

Hidden Triggers

Imagine that your partner makes a seemingly small comment, like, *"You didn't load the dishwasher again?"* And even though they didn't raise their voice, your chest tightens defensively. You feel dismissed. Judged. Disrespected. And before you can stop yourself, you snap.

That's a trigger. Not the dishwasher. Not the comment. But the comment stirred something inside you.

Triggers are like invisible bruises. You may not even know they're there until someone presses on one and suddenly, you react. Not because the person did something terrible, but because something inside you flared up fast.

We all carry triggers. They come from many places- past relationships, childhood, burnout, overstimulation, or simply being stretched too thin for too long. Parental fears, like not being good enough or concerns over emotional safety (being accepted for who you are), also contribute significantly to hidden triggers.

In this book, we will focus solely on **parenting triggers.**

Here's the truth: It's not just your child's behavior that sets you off. It's how you experience and interpret that behavior.

 Exercise: Identify Your Parental Triggers

1. What are the moments that make your whole body tighten?
2. What actions from your child make you go from calm to boiling?
   - When your child talks back?
   - When they cry for no reason?
   - When they ignore your instructions?
   - When they interrupt you just as you finally sit down?

Your reactions aren't random. They're not about you being "too emotional" or "too sensitive." They're signs that something deeper is being stirred.

Maybe your child's backtalk makes you feel disrespected—not just now, but in the same way you felt dismissed growing up.

Maybe their crying makes you feel helpless because your parents or guardians didn't make space for your feelings.

Perhaps your child's resistance makes you feel out of control, and that terrifies you.

Your Child's Behavior Lights the Fuse

When we take the time to check our emotions and the actions that arise from them, we create space for ourselves. And that space? That's where new possibilities start.

Examining the motivations behind your anger isn't about blaming your past. Doing so allows you to better understand your present. Because once you realize, *"Oh! This isn't just about my kid throwing toys—this is about me feeling powerless again,"* you're no longer reacting blindly. You're parenting with awareness.

If you've ever wondered, "Why did I react like that?" then this next part is for you.

 ***Exercise: Moving from Reaction to Reflection***

Here's a small practice you can use when you feel your anger rise:

Take a pause, breathe, and ask yourself:

- What just triggered me?
- Does this moment remind me of something else?
- What am I really feeling underneath this anger?

Just asking these questions is a powerful first step. You can't avoid your triggers, but you *can* meet them with curiosity instead of shame. Doing so allows you to shift from reacting to reflecting. That's how you begin to become the parent you want to be. It all starts by noticing what's really going on beneath the surface.

More Pressure, Less Support

There's an African proverb that states: *"It takes a village to raise a child."* But for many parents today, that village feels non-existent, or much smaller than it was in past generations.

You might be parenting without having grandparents nearby, without close friends who can show up in a crisis, without a partner who fully understands your mental load, or even without a partner at all. If any of these scenarios resonate with you, then you may feel like there isn't one moment in the day that is truly yours, especially if you have younger children.

You love your child deeply. You try your best to do right by them. You pour your energy into being present, patient, and kind. But some days, it all feels too heavy. You snap. You shut down. You yell. And later, you feel terrible.

You wonder, *"Why can't I hold it together like other parents do?"*

Here's the thing: It's not just you. Parenting has always been hard. But modern parenting? It's a whole different kind of hard.

You're taking on the work of a village—without a village. You're raising a child in a world filled with noise: advice overload, social media comparisons, and the pressure to meet impossible parenting standards. These pressures can lead to a constant state of anxiety and guilt, making you feel like you're not living up to societal expectations. Combine all of this with being told that if you yell, if your child misbehaves, or if you feel overwhelmed, it's your fault.

In today's fast-paced culture, there's an unseen race to achieve parenting milestones quickly and perfectly. This fear is worsened by the constant flow of parenting advice, which encourages you to do more and to do it flawlessly. Driven by the fear of not being enough, you may feel compelled to accelerate your child's learning to match with that of their peers, focusing on their achievements without recognizing the importance of nurturing their emotional well-being.

Great Expectations

A generation ago, many parents had a built-in community. They had family and friends to step in when they were tapped out. They had someone to say, "I've got this. Go rest." But now? We're raising children in isolation (relatively speaking) and are expected to fulfill every need without breaking.

While parental support systems have noticeably declined in recent times, parental expectations have increased significantly. You're told to be calm but firm, gentle but in control. Always be available to your child while also fostering their independence. Every scroll on your phone advises you of what you *should* be doing, and every meltdown or hard moment makes you feel like you're falling short.

You love your child with all your heart, but the pressure of becoming a perfect parent can feel overwhelming. You're not just trying to manage tantrums; you might be juggling overstimulation, emotional labor, sleep deprivation, financial worries, and the silent weight of *trying so hard to do it right.* If it feels like it is too much, that's because it often is.

Are You Stuck in the Yelling Cycle?

You yell. Then you feel guilty. So, you soften. Apologize. Perhaps offer a snack, a treat, or an extra 10 minutes of screen time—something to smooth over the tension.

You don't do this because you're manipulative. You do this because you love your child and hate how things just turned out. You want to make it right, reconnect, and let them know that they're still deeply loved. So, you reach for something—*anything*—that might bring you both back to peace, alleviate your guilt, and make them feel better in the moment.

This is where many parents find themselves, time and over again: **The yelling-guilt-gift cycle.**

Yell → Guilt → Make up for it → Repeat.

Here's how that might play out in real life:

- "I shouldn't have snapped. I'll take them out for an ice cream."
- "I feel awful. I'll let them stay up a little longer."
- "I want them to know I love them. Maybe this will help."

Your heart is in the right place, but over time, this well-intentioned pattern can create confusion. Children don't learn to take responsibility for their misbehavior when they are rewarded for it.

They learn that outbursts are followed by treats or leniency. As a result, instead of feeling more in control, you feel even more stuck.

Why is it so Hard to Stop the Cycle?

Here's why it's so difficult to break the yelling cycle:

In the short term, yelling feels effective. Your child freezes, listens to you, and backs down. For a moment, you feel in control and relieved. But then the guilt hits. You remember that you don't want to be the kind of parent whose first instinct is to yell. Still, in that heated moment, yelling seemed to *work*. It gave you a quick sense of control.

And that relief? Your brain notices it and starts to reinforce the pattern.

This is when you should pause and observe how patterns form:

- A behavior triggers you.
- You explode.
- You feel awful and overcorrect.
- The child learns: "If things escalate, something soft comes after."

- And next time? It happens again because neither of you learned what to do instead.

Just like that, you're stuck in a loop of your own creation that you never intended to create. This cycle continues, as parents may feel that they are failing in rectifying a tense situation if they don't provide immediate comfort or reward.

Exploring the root of your anger isn't meant to make you feel shame or guilt. This kind of introspective self-discovery allows you to break the cycle.

Parenting in Survival Mode

You yell more, snap faster, and feel like you're always on edge. Later, you crash into guilt, wondering, *"Why am I like this?"*

"Survival parenting" is when you're no longer parenting with intention; you're just trying to get through the day. You wake up already overwhelmed. Your goal for the day isn't to thrive; it's to manage the next meltdown, the next mess, the next hour. You're not thinking long-term. You're just thinking, *"How am I going to make it to bedtime?"*

When you're in this state, you're constantly reacting instead of responding. You're maxed out, pulled in many directions, and it's not your fault.

Fears about not being enough, combined with a lack of emotional safety at home, can keep you stuck in a state of survival mode. When you're constantly reacting, not reflecting, there's little room to feel safe enough to pause, breathe, and parent with intention. A simple "no" from your child sounds like defiance. A tantrum feels like a personal attack. Suddenly, you're yelling—not because you wanted to, but because it exploded out of you. This happens when your nervous system is constantly in a state of high alert. You're not parenting with presence; you're parenting with adrenaline. And when you're constantly alert, there's no space to pause. Only to survive.

From Panic to Presence: One Shift at a Time

When your body is in survival mode, even the smallest challenge feels like it's too much. You're not lazy, you're overwhelmed, and anger becomes your autopilot.

So, what helps? **Noticing.**

Noticing doesn't fix everything. But it opens a door.

So, the next time you feel the heat rising, take a breath and whisper to yourself: *"I'm in survival mode right now."* That gentle pause can shift your mental state from reaction to reflection.

This pause will give you the space to make seemingly small but incredibly impactful changes. Some of the scenarios mentioned below may seem familiar to you; some may not. But in each case, acknowledge that you're in survival mode, take a breath, and give yourself the space to make one small change.

- *Scenario 1: Say no to something that drains you.*

It's Tuesday night, and you've had a long day at work. You've just finished the dishes and tidied up the house. Suddenly, your child wants to create a volcano using baking soda. You know from previous experience that this activity requires patience, time, and a significant amount of cleanup. Your first instinct might be to say something like, "I've just spent an hour cooking and cleaning, and you want to make a mess?" Instead, pause and breathe. You might try, "That's a great idea. Gather the materials that you need, and we can do this tomorrow evening."

- *Scenario 2: Ask for help.*

You've chosen to take an hour-long exercise every Monday evening, but your partner has to work late. You have a trusted friend who lives nearby and has offered to watch your child in a pinch many times, but you've never taken them up on it. Instead of missing your class and silently resenting your child, you can ask your friend for help. They can eat pizza and watch a movie, and you can return from your class feeling refreshed.

- *Scenario 3: Relive the moment.*

Your child slams the door and yells, "You never listen!" Instead of reacting without thought, remind yourself: "This isn't about me. This is a sign they're overwhelmed." You take a deep breath, lower your voice, and say, "Let's try again when we're both calm."

Now, spend 5 minutes thinking of a scenario that could trigger you by following these steps:

1) Write down the scenario.
2) Add how you might initially react when anger takes over.
3) Then add how you would like to respond.
4) Finally, write down a plan for how you'll get there.

Even slight shifts in attitude and action can start to break the cycle. You don't need a new routine. You need a new rhythm—one that honors the fact that *you're human, too.* You won't escape survival mode overnight. But you can step out of it moment by moment. Not by yelling less, but by understanding what the yelling is trying to tell you.

That's how real change begins: Quietly, and with the choice to pause instead of reacting.

What's Your Default Reaction?

When your child refuses to listen, talks back, or throws something across the room, what do you usually do? Raise your voice? Shut down and go silent? Walk away in silent anger? Or sink into guilt and tears once the dust settles?

Every parent has a go-to reaction—a way your body and mind respond when things feel too big, too loud, or too intense. These reactions aren't random. They're shaped by years of experience.

Do you know your default reactions? Write them down and face them head on. Some of these situations might resonate with you, or they might prompt you to think of your own.

- You yell because it was the only way you were ever heard.
- You freeze because, in your past, expressing emotion didn't feel safe.
- You micromanage because unpredictability causes your chest to tighten with fear.

These patterns are shaped by how we were raised, how overwhelmed we feel now, and whether we believe anyone is in our corner when we're struggling.

You don't choose these reactions on purpose, and that might make you feel powerless. However, you *do* have the power to address the root of these reactions and create new patterns.

Noticing is the First Step

You can't permanently change your perspective and default reactions overnight. That's ok. Acknowledging your triggers and making space to improve is where you can start to manifest real and tangible progress. By being aware and observant of yourself, you begin to understand what lies underneath and deal with it.

Think about when people choose to lose weight or make a monumental shift in behavior that is hard but healthy. The decision to act is usually deliberate and not taken casually.

One day, they look in the mirror and notice their face looks chubbier, or their favorite jeans, the ones that had fit perfectly last year, feel tight. They decide they're tired of feeling powerless and plan to act and make a change.

They noticed something, and that noticing is the turning point.

✎   Grab a pen and paper and write down answers to these questions:

- When I feel pushed, do I get louder or feel smaller?

- Are there certain behaviors—whining, lying, defiance—that trigger my anger faster than others?

- Do I feel helpless, ashamed, or out of control in those moments?

When you name your default reactions, you create a space to recognize **what your triggers are and how you respond to them.**

And that space? **That's where your power lies.** Often, these default reactions are deeply linked to unaddressed fears and a lack of emotional safety. If you understand the connections between your triggers and your initial negative responses, you give yourself the power to create more intentional responses.

Parent Perspective: *"It wasn't about the spilled juice. It was about me feeling like no one sees how much I do. That's what made me yell."*

This kind of self-awareness and insight doesn't erase the outburst—but it could help prevent the next one.

Chapter 1 recap:

Why You Really Yell

1. **Yelling usually isn't about your child**; it's about your own hidden stress, exhaustion, and past experiences.

2. **Modern parenting piles on unrealistic expectations** and isolates you from real support.

3. Take the time to **identify your parenting triggers**.

4. Identifying your parenting triggers and your default reactions to stressful situations is the first step toward change. **Awareness creates space** for new behavioral responses.

CHAPTER 2

THE ANGER UNDERNEATH

*"Your triggers are your responsibility.
It isn't your child's job to regulate your emotions."* – Rebecca Eanes

The Anger Iceberg

You probably know this moment well: Your child slams a door, talks back, or refuses to listen. You suddenly feel the heat rise inside you. You yell. Maybe you slam something too. Then you walk away feeling awful and confused, asking yourself, "Why did I get so upset over something so small?"

That's the thing about anger—it often shows up loud and fast, but it rarely travels alone. Fear, self-doubt, and insecurity are often it's co-passengers, quietly riding along. They may not be the first thing you see, but they're often what's really driving your reaction.

Anger is what appears on the outside. But underneath? There's always more. Think of anger like an iceberg. The part you see above the water—the yelling, snapping, eye-rolling—is just the tip of the iceberg. Beneath are the real emotions, those "co-passengers" of exhaustion, shame, fear, feeling unheard, helplessness, guilt, and remorse.

You're not yelling about the toys scattered on the floor. You're yelling because you feel like no one listens to you. Because you're overwhelmed and haven't had a break in days. Because you grew up walking on eggshells, and now, your child's chaos triggers panic in your body.

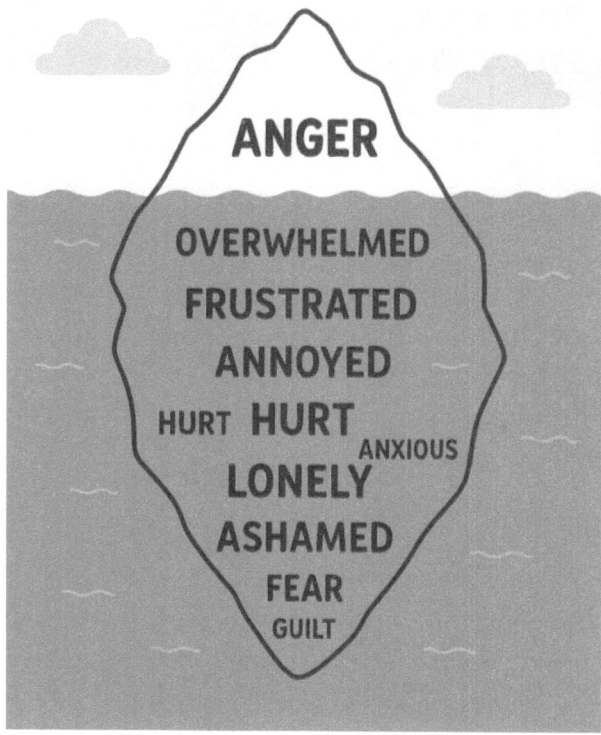

Wiring, Not Weakness

When you react with anger, you're relying on an old defense mechanism. Anger has a seemingly protective quality. It steps in when the softer parts of us—like sadness, vulnerability, or fear—don't feel safe enough to come out. That's why we react with a raised voice instead of saying, *"I'm scared you're not okay,"* or *"I feel alone in this,"* or *"I'm not sure how to handle what's happening."* It's not weakness—it's wiring.

This isn't just an emotional theory; this is how your nervous system works, and it's backed by science.

Your brain is wired to protect you. When it senses a threat, even something as small as your child's defiance, it reacts quickly, saying: **Defend. Control. Fix.**

This kind of instant, life-saving defense was necessary when our ancestors faced the dangers of the wild. Although we have evolved, our brains don't always distinguish between real danger and emotional discomfort. It senses distress and triggers immediate action.

That's why your child whining about more screen time or throwing a tantrum can make your heart race and push your body into the red zone. Unless you pause, that impulse drives everything. When we don't slow down to look underneath the surface, we end up reacting from the tip of the iceberg. We yell. We punish. Not because we're bad parents, but because we're overwhelmed and hurting.

But there's good news—you have the power to redirect those impulses.

Naming Leads To Taming:
Anger Isn't A Character Flaw. It's A Signal

Anger is your body's way of saying, *"Something inside me needs care."* And that's something you can work with. The more curious you become about your anger, the more you pause and wonder, *"What's really going on here?"*, the less power it has over you. The more power you gain, the more you're able to respond with intention instead of impulse.

Here's a practice you can try next time you feel the heat rising:

Pause. Picture the iceberg. Ask yourself: What might be underneath this? It could be:

- "I feel unappreciated."
- "I'm exhausted."
- "This reminds me of how I was treated as a kid."
- "I'm scared I'm messing this up."

Whatever it is, name it. Even silently. Because naming is the first step to taming. And when you address the emotion underneath, you won't explode from the one on the top.

Your anger isn't something to be ashamed of. It's a signal that something important to you is being threatened, and the fact that you feel it shows how deeply you care.

Are You Repeating or Repairing?

Imagine you're in the middle of a hard parenting moment. Your child is melting down, the noise is intense, and suddenly, you hear yourself shout, "Stop crying! You're being ridiculous!" And the moment those words leave your mouth, your stomach drops. *Did I really just say that? That's what my mom used to say to me.*

You swore you'd never do this. You promised yourself you'd be different, gentler, kinder, more understanding.

And yet, here they are again: the words, the tone, the energy you thought you'd left behind. It hits hard.

Parent Perspective: *"I didn't even realize I was doing it,"* one mom told me. *"Until one day I yelled, and it was her voice—not mine—that came out of my mouth."*

We love our parents. We know they did their best for us. But we also carry the pain of their imperfection. Often, the things that hurt us the most as children are the very things we unconsciously repeat when we're overwhelmed.

Letting Go of Blame, Breaking Patterns

We all enter parenthood with a subconscious blueprint shaped by our upbringing. Sometimes we repeat what we have experienced. Sometimes we run in the opposite direction. But either way, our childhood silently shapes our responses when parenting gets hard.

Even if your childhood wasn't traumatic, it left imprints on you. When your child's big feelings show up, they often hit the parts of you that never received support or comfort. The bruises we talked about in Chapter 1 are pressed all over again.

That doesn't mean something is wrong with you. It means you're still carrying wounds that didn't heal.

Healing doesn't mean pointing fingers or exploring every wound in detail. It means being honest about the fact that some parts of us still hurt. It means recognizing when an old pattern shows up—not to shame ourselves, but to understand why it persists. Healing is silently saying to your child, *"This was passed down to me, but I don't have to pass it on to you."*

That's what healing, or repair, looks like: To pause and breathe. To step out of your patterns and say something new in a moment when you were once silenced.

Parent Perspective: *A mother told me, "I realized I was yelling at my son for crying over small things because I grew up hearing, 'Toughen up.'"* However, she noticed that for the first time when she knelt beside him and said, 'It's okay to cry. I'm here,' she felt something positive shift in herself and her child.

This is how the cycle breaks. Not through perfection, but through presence. Through small, brave choices. You aren't just parenting; **you're acknowledging your story and writing the next chapter.**

What You're Carrying, And What You're Passing On

We often think about the physical traits that we pass down to our kids—eye color, curls, or the way they laugh. But we also pass down something far less visible, and sometimes far more powerful: **our emotional inheritance.**

You can't always see it clearly, but it shows up in how you react to tears, in the pressure to stay "fine," and the urge to fix instead of understanding them. When you become aware of what has shaped you, you can choose what to keep and what to gently let go of.

Every home has unspoken rules about emotions. You might not remember the exact words, but you remember how they made you feel. What was allowed, what was avoided, and what was never spoken?

Perhaps in your family, anger was expressed through yelling or silence. Sadness was ignored. Asking for help made you feel like you were a burden. Being "good" meant staying quiet and easy.

You probably have adapted by following these rules. You have buried emotions. You have over-functioned while taking care of everyone else's needs and ignoring your own. You became the one who held it all together, even when it felt overwhelming.

Parent Perspective: *"I don't know why my son's crying makes me so mad. I think it's because I was always told that crying was a sign of weakness. So, it triggers something I have never healed."*

That's emotional inheritance in real time. While you can't change your past, you *can* change how it shapes your present and your future.

This emotional inheritance often feeds into our fears as parents. Perhaps your upbringing left you with a fear of not being enough, driving a relentless urge to overcompensate in your own parenting. It's important to remember that yelling—often fueled by anxieties about our child's future or our own insecurities—can undermine a family's emotional safety.

Your child might feel attacked instead of loved, leading to emotional detachment. That's why it's essential to address your fears constructively to create and nurture a safe, supportive environment.

The path forward involves acknowledging that emotional inheritance isn't static; it's learned, and what's learned can be unlearned. Start by recognizing any emotional neglect you might have experienced.

Break this cycle by providing validation and understanding to your child and their emotions. Learn to enjoy the highs and face the lows head-on, and with compassion. Foster a nurturing environment where your child feels safe to show you their true selves without fear of reprimand or judgment.

We don't need to be healed to offer healing. By modeling emotional safety—even as we continue our own journey—we build the kind of home we once longed for. By choosing to do something different, we give our children the very kind of compassion and understanding that we're learning to give ourselves.

When one person chooses to do something different, cycles can begin to shift. You can't heal your relationships all at once, but slowly, gently, with love, effort, and truth. Each intentional moment becomes a stepping stone toward a more compassionate future.

✏️ Quiz: Identify Your Triggers

The sun is shining, the birds are chirping, and you're ready to greet the new day. Your 8-year-old wants to play Minecraft. Your toddler refuses breakfast, and your partner leaves for work without a word.

Suddenly, you snap. Not because your children are being difficult, but because *something inside you* just overflowed.

That "something" is an example of a parenting trigger, which we covered in Chapter 1: an old wound, an unmet need, or a story you've carried for years. The more clearly you can name it, the more power you gain to pause, choose differently, and break the pattern—for both you and your child.

The following quiz isn't about judgment. It's about building curiosity, awareness, and self-compassion. Take a breath. Be honest with yourself—not to shame, but to understand.

✏️ Which of these triggers cause you to yell or shut down?

(Check all that apply.)

☐ Running late or feeling rushed.

☐ Being ignored after giving multiple instructions.

- ☐ Noise, mess, or visual clutter.
- ☐ Constant interruptions.
- ☐ Backtalk, whining, or tone.
- ☐ Feeling like you're doing everything alone.
- ☐ Seeing your child behave like your younger self.
- ☐ Last-minute changes or lack of control.
- ☐ Feeling invisible, disrespected, or dismissed.
- ☐ When your child expresses "too much" emotion.

Now write and reflect:

- What do these triggers have in common?
- Are they tied to your **childhood experiences**, your **expectations**, or your **unmet needs**? Or are they tied to something else altogether?
- Which triggers occur most often and when? (e.g., after a bad sleep? After work? During transitions?)

What To Do Next?

You can't eliminate your triggers, but you can build awareness around them so that you respond with more intention and less shame. When you can pause and say, *"Oh, this is that feeling again"*—you've already made a shift.

You've created just enough space to choose something new. This isn't failure, it's growth. You're a parent with patterns. And change happens when you name these patterns.

Chapter 2 Recap:
The Anger Underneath

1. **Anger rarely comes from the moment you are in;** it emerges when something underneath is triggered.

2. **Big feelings** like shame, fear, guilt, and helplessness often **wear the mask of anger.** When we explode, it's often because in our past, we didn't feel safe to show those emotions.

3. **Your childhood shaped more than your memories—it shaped your patterns.** Recognizing what you inherited emotionally helps you choose what to carry forward (and what to gently let go of).

4. You're not failing as a parent. You're simply repeating what feels familiar. *But **familiar doesn't mean final.***

CHAPTER 3

KNOW YOUR PARENTING STYLE

"The way we talk to our children becomes their inner voice."
– Peggy O'Mara

What's Your Parenting Style?

It's very likely that your parents didn't think about their parenting style, nor did their parents before them. Maybe your parents were strict and controlling. Maybe they were permissive and inconsistent. Maybe you never quite knew what version of them you'd see depending on their mood, stress, or exhaustion.

Then you became a parent. And unintentionally, those same patterns started showing up in your behavior—especially during moments of stress.

You're not alone. Many parents experience the same thing. That's why it's important to understand your parenting style. Why? Not to label yourself or judge how you were raised. But to understand: *Why do I react this way?* And *how does my way of parenting affect my child emotionally?*

✏ Grab a pen and reflect on these questions:

- What is my parenting style?
- What kind of parenting did I grow up with?
- How might those experiences shape my responses toward my child?

Your parenting style isn't just about rules or routines. It's about how you handle stress, how you connect with your child, how you set boundaries, and how your child feels on the other side of all that.

In this chapter, we'll explore 3 common parenting styles—not to limit you, but to help you understand the patterns behind your reactions. Most of us are a blend, but recognizing your dominant style can help you grow in awareness of not just of how you parent, but also of how your child experiences you.

This goal here isn't to pick one parenting label for yourself, but knowing the main types may help you to understand your natural tendencies, allowing you to parent with more clarity and awareness.

The Authoritative Parent: Clear and Connected

The authoritative parent leads with both love and structure. They set limits, but do so with warmth. They don't just stop their child's misbehavior; they also stay connected while it's happening.

Parenting Scenario: Your 9-year-old slams their bedroom door after you ask them to get off the tablet. You feel the urge to yell back or take it away for a week. Instead, you take a breath and say:

"I know you're frustrated, but slamming doors isn't okay. Let's take a break and talk about a better way to handle this."

You hold the boundary, but you foster connection by helping your child learn to manage their big emotions with your support.

Authoritative parents provide emotional safety while maintaining firm boundaries. Their children feel guided, not controlled, because they understand that putting a limit doesn't mean disconnection. Kids raised this way usually feel safe expressing big emotions because they know their parents can handle it and still stay close.

The Permissive Parent: Big on Love, Light on Limits

This parent is deeply nurturing. They value connection and want their child to feel loved no matter what. However, when it comes to setting or holding boundaries, they often struggle.

Instead of saying: *"We don't hit,"* they might say: *"Please don't hit, okay? That makes Mommy sad."*

When the child's misbehavior continues, the parent may sigh and walk away, unsure of what else to do. These parents usually come from a heartfelt place: *"I don't want to be the parent who scared me."*

Without clear limits, kids can feel emotionally unanchored. They may act out more, not because they're "bad," but because they're unsure of what's okay and what isn't.

The Reactive Parent: Just Burned Out

This final parenting style isn't really a "style;" it's a **state**. If you're a reactive parent, you aren't lazy or mean—it's just that you've reached your limits. You start the day with the best intentions. But when the milk spills, your child screams "No!" for the fifth time, you suddenly explode.

Instead of calmly saying, *"I won't let you talk to me like that,"* it comes out as:

"What is wrong with you? Why are you always like this?"

You're not trying to shame your child. You're just emotionally spent.

Reactive parenting occurs when your nervous system gets exhausted. When you're overstretched, overwhelmed, and under-supported, your brain does what it knows—it protects. Sometimes that protection shows up as yelling, shutting down, or saying things you don't mean.

This doesn't mean you don't love your child. It means you've hit the edge of your window of tolerance, and your nervous system has gone into survival mode.

THE AUTHORITATIVE PARENT

LOVE + LIMITS

THE PERMISSIVE PARENT

LOVE - LIMITS

THE REACTIVE PARENT

STRESS, NO REGULATIONS

Your Parenting Style Sends a Message

Now that you have a clearer sense of how you tend to show up—whether it's with structure, softness, or stress, it's time to ask yourself a deeper question:

What is your parenting style teaching your child?

Whether you realize it or not, **you're always sending a message to your child.** Not just with your words, but with your tone, your follow-through, and your responses when things go wrong.

You might wonder, "Am I messing this all up?" You're not. Recognizing your parenting style and how you can improve it doesn't mean you have to strive for constant perfection. It's about understanding what those silent messages are saying and working to improve the communication.

Here's what those silent messages might be saying to your child:

- A parent who says, *"I love you,"* but often yells or withdraws: **"Love is unpredictable."**
- A parent who avoids setting limits to maintain peace: **"Your big feelings are in charge. I can't handle them."**
- A parent who stays warm and calm even while holding a boundary: **"You're safe, even when things are hard. I'm not going anywhere."**

None of these messages comes from bad intentions. They come from exhaustion, anxiety, or fear. However, children absorb them deeply. What they absorb doesn't just shape their behavior; it shapes their perception of themselves and impacts how they navigate the world.

If they receive consistent love, they believe they're worthy. If they absorb chaos, they may believe they're too much to handle. If they see that love disappears when they misbehave, they may believe, **"My parents' love depends on how I act. I'd better stay small to stay safe."**

One of the most powerful parenting truths is this:

Kids don't need you to get it right every time. They just need you to be steady enough so that they know what to expect.

Does this scenario ring a bell? On Monday evening, you say, "No snacks before dinner." On Tuesday, you give in. On Wednesday, you yell about it.

In this scenario, your child isn't just confused; they're unsettled. Unpredictability doesn't feel safe, but consistency does.

Now imagine this scenario instead: Your child asks for a snack before dinner. You calmly say, "No snacks before dinner." They whine. You empathize but hold the boundary repeatedly. Over time, they stop testing you. Not because they love the rule, but because they trust you.

Your unspoken message to them becomes: **"You can push, and I won't fall apart. I've got us."**

What Does Your Child Need from You?

We've talked about how your parenting style sends a message even when you are unaware of it. So, what kind of message helps a child feel safe, confident, and connected?

Your child doesn't need perfect scripts or calm voices all the time. What your child needs the most is a parent who keeps showing up with the following:

- **Love and support**: Give them your love, not only when they behave well, but also when they're melting down or falling apart. Unconditional love is the anchor that helps kids feel safe enough to grow.

- **Consistency and predictability**: The world is an unpredictable place. Kids thrive when they know what to expect. When you're steady with limits, boundaries, and your tone, it helps your child feel grounded, regardless of the situation.

- **Patience and forgiveness**: Your child is still learning, and so are you. Grace and repair matter more than getting it right the first time.

- **Encouragement and empowerment**: Kids rise to meet the expectations of the adults who believe in them. When you say, *"You've got this, and I've got you,"* they begin to believe in themselves.

You don't need to do everything perfectly. What matters is the direction you're moving in, not whether you get it right every time. The more you show up with love, clarity, and steadiness, the more your child will learn: *"I'm safe, I'm loved, and I'm not alone."*

That's the kind of message that lasts a lifetime.

Chapter 3 Recap:

Know Your Parenting Style

1. **Your parenting style is more than just a label.** It's a pattern shaped by stress, your childhood experiences, and instinct; recognizing yours can help you break old patterns.

2. There are **3 common parenting styles**: **authoritative** parenting balances warmth and structure. **Permissive** and **reactive** parenting styles often come from a place of love, but lack the proper amount of limits and/or regulation that your child needs

3. **Your parenting style sends a message to your child** not just through your words, but through your tone, follow-through, and presence.

4. **Kids thrive when parents lead with clarity, emotional safety, and consistent connection.**

5. You don't need to (and can't be!) be perfect. You just need to **move in a new, positive direction**, recognizing your patterns and adjusting your behavior to meet your child where they are.

Stay Calm, Take Control
Part II

CHAPTER 4

THE CALM STARTS WITH YOU

"Peace begins with me." – Louise Hay

Reaction Vs. Response

You ask your child to put on their shoes. They don't move. You ask again, this time louder. Still nothing. Then something inside you snaps, and suddenly, you hear your voice booming through the hallway: **"Why can't you just listen?!"**

That, right there, is a reaction.

Reactions are often impulsive, emotional, and stem from exhaustion, stress, or overwhelm. Reacting might make you feel guilty—not because your feelings are "wrong," but because the way they spilled out didn't feel aligned with the parent you want to be.

Now, let's replay the above scenario. This time, you *respond* instead of *reacting*:

You feel the frustration rise. You pause and breathe. You walk over to your child, crouch down to their level, and say, *"I know it's hard to stop playing. But it's time to go. Let me help you put on your shoes."*

That's a response. The difference between a reaction and a response is this:

Reactions are automatic. Responses are intentional.

Intention, Not Perfection

The difference between reacting and responding isn't about perfection; it's about intention. The former is driven by raw emotion, while the latter is guided by presence and awareness.

Here's the part most parents never hear enough: your reactions aren't a personal failure. You're not overreacting because you're too emotional or bad at parenting.

Reactions are the patterns created in your nervous system, deeply ingrained responses that are shaped by your stress levels, your upbringing, and the support you're getting (or not getting) while parenting. When your nervous system is under pressure, it follows the path it knows the best. Reactions become like grooves in your brain—automatic tracks your mind runs on. Unless you start to notice these grooves and act on them, they will continue to influence your behavior.

That's why the first step toward change isn't to "just calm down" (If only it were that easy, right?) The real first step is simply noticing. Pause in that heated moment and say to yourself, *"Whoa. I'm about to snap."*

That small moment of awareness, as simple as it sounds, is where the shift begins.

Responding (Not Reacting) Builds Emotional Safety

Emotional regulation or "responding" isn't just a gift for you—it becomes a gift for your child, too.

You may achieve short-term results by *reacting*. Your child may stop the misbehavior, clean up the mess, or fall in line. However, when you *respond* with intention, you build something far more important—long-term trust.

When your child observes that you don't fall apart when they do, they believe that you're not just managing a tough moment, you're creating safety.

Through your presence, you're silently telling your child, *"You don't have to be perfect for me to stay connected to you."* Over time, that message becomes their inner voice. It becomes their anchor when life gets hard and they believe: *"I'm still loved, even when I struggle."*

Such a response doesn't come from perfection. It comes from practice—from noticing when you're overwhelmed, from pausing just long enough to choose a different response, and from remembering that even one breath, taken with awareness, can change the moment. A breath that says, *"I don't have to react impulsively."* A pause that says, *"I can lead from connection, not control."* That's where real change begins. Not just in your child, but in you as well.

Why "Just Breathe" Isn't Enough

You're in the middle of a tough situation. The baby is crying. Your toddler has just dumped an entire box of cereal on the floor. Your 7-year-old is yelling that socks are "the worst thing ever invented!" Just as your nervous system is about to snap, your partner calmly says, **"Relax, take a breath."**

And in that moment, you want to scream.

Intentional breathing can be incredibly powerful. However, most people overlook that intentional breathing is more than just taking a breath. It's about **how** you breathe, **when** you breathe, and **what you believe** while breathing. A single shallow breath won't calm your system if you're already overwhelmed and in the fight-or-flight mode.

Why It Feels So Hard To "Just Breathe"

We have briefly discussed this in the previous chapters, but it's worth repeating. When you're triggered, your nervous system flips into high alert. Your heart races. Your muscles tighten. Your brain's logic center, the prefrontal cortex, goes offline. Your survival brain, the amygdala, takes over.

In this state, your body is incapable of resolving a conflict calmly. It's preparing to fight, flee, or freeze, as if you're facing danger. It takes **intentional nervous system care** to bring your body back to a state of safety. So yes, breathing matters, but real regulation takes more than inhaling and exhaling air.

What Actually Helps

Here's what calms your body and helps you respond instead of reacting:

- **Grounded breath:**
    - Inhale slowly through your nose for 4 seconds.
    - Exhale through your mouth for 6 seconds.
    - Repeat thrice.

This rhythm tells your brain: *We're safe. We can settle.*

- **Anchor phrase:** As you exhale, try pairing your breath with a calming message that you say silently to yourself. Something simple and grounding like:

    "I'm safe."

    "This is hard, but I can handle it."

    "My child needs help, not hurt."

This practice reminds your body of your ability to choose differently.

- **Body scan:** A body scan is a powerful tool that can simultaneously **calm** both your mind and body.

Here's how it works:

In a seated position or while lying down, inhale through your nose and exhale through your mouth. Repeat this until you feel more relaxed. Ask yourself: Where am I holding tension? Can I drop my shoulders? Unclench my jaw? Let my belly soften?

Even small physical shifts like these can signal your brain, *"We're okay. We don't need to be on high alert."*

Grounded breath, anchor phrases, and body scans help calm your nervous system. They are incredibly beneficial for both your body and mind. These are small practices that make a big difference—particularly in the messiest moments.

When You Notice, You Create Space

Parent Perspectives:

- *"When I feel the volcano rising inside me, I put my hand on my chest and say, 'You're okay.' It felt strange at first, but it helped. That one moment of calm kept me from saying something I'd regret."*

- *"I used to think I had to be calm to parent well. Now I know I just have to find calm in the moment, even for ten seconds."*

And yes, it's okay to take a moment for yourself in the bathroom or the laundry room, or with your eyes closed for a few seconds while your child melts down in front of you. This is how you build emotional regulation: not by pretending you're fine, but by signaling your body and brain that you are safe enough to slow down.

Here's the hidden gift in all of this: When your child sees you pause, breathe, and reset—even once—they learn to do the same. They learn that big feelings don't have to lead to big explosions. They learn that calm is a choice that they can make, not something they're born with.

Emotional Regulation

Let's be real: Staying calm in the middle of chaos isn't just hard. Sometimes it feels downright impossible.

Picture this: You've had a long day at work and barely made it home in time to start dinner, which is now burning on the stove. You're running late for soccer practice, and your 8-year-old can't find her cleats. Then your partner calls and says they have a flat tire, and you'll need to pick them up.

You know you're *supposed* to stay calm in the storm, but in that moment, your body feels like it's on fire. Your heart is pounding, your muscles tighten, and all you want is for something, anything, to just stop.

What does emotional regulation really mean in moments like these?

Let's start with what emotional regulation **doesn't** mean:

- It **doesn't** mean suppressing your feelings or pretending you're fine.

- It doesn't mean becoming a robot who never gets frustrated or flustered.

- And it *definitely* doesn't mean holding it all in until you explode later.

Emotional regulation means staying present, even when your emotions are intense. It means pausing to notice what's happening in your body—the tight jaw, the racing thoughts, the urge to yell. Instead, you choose to ground yourself before you react. You're choosing how to respond, rather than reacting with panic or overwhelm.

Regulation In Real Life

Let's talk about practicing emotional regulation during real, messy moments:

You ask your child to put down the video game controller because it's time for dinner. Instead, they choose to throw it across the room and refuse to eat. Your first instinct is to react quickly, perhaps by punishing or yelling. Instead, you check yourself, repeat your anchor phrase silently, and calmly state: "I'm not going to yell. As I said, it's time for dinner. Pick up the controller and come upstairs. If you don't, there will be consequences."

Feeling proud of yourself but still feeling like you might explode, you walk to the kitchen, open the freezer, and grab a handful of ice. You let the shock of the cold bring you back to your body, back to the moment.

Training your brain to respond emotionally isn't easy, especially if no one modeled this behavior when you were growing up. Here's the good news: Every time you practice emotional regulation, it gets easier and creates a habit.

Parent Perspective: *One mom told me she kept a sticky note on the fridge that said, "Pause. Breathe. Choose." "It sounds silly, but it saved me from screaming at least 3 times a week."*

You don't always have to be perfectly calm. You just have to be aware enough to notice the heat rising inside you, then take the next step without fueling it.

What You Expect, You Create

There's a quiet truth in parenting that's easy to miss, but once you see it, you can't ignore it: the self-fulfilling prophecy. What you expect from and project to your child, good or bad, can lead to that expected outcome.

If you say something multiple times, even if it's not true, it can become reality:

"She never listens."

"He's always defiant."

"They just don't care."

In the moment, your thoughts feel right. You're not imagining things. You've seen the behavior enough times to believe it. It starts to feel like a fact.

When we expect certain patterns, we often start reacting as if they're already happening, even if they aren't. And those preloaded reactions? They can actually bring out the behavior in our child, even when it wasn't there to begin with.

Children are incredibly responsive to the energy we bring into the room.

Let's walk through how this plays out.

You expect your child to talk back. Maybe it happens so often that you're bracing for it before they even speak. The moment they do, your body tenses. Your voice sharpens. You're already on edge, preparing for a battle that hasn't even started.

And your child? They feel that tension, too. Even if you don't say a word, they pick up on your tone, posture, and vibe, and it puts them in a defensive mode. Then they do exactly what you anticipated: They talk back.

Now you're both stuck in a vicious cycle that neither of you wanted. Not because you're a bad parent. Not because they're a difficult child. But because **expectation shapes perception, and perception shapes reaction.**

This doesn't mean you need to pretend your child is perfect or ignore their challenging behavior. It means that when you shift your expectations, you begin to shift the reaction that you invite. And that shift changes everything.

You pause a little longer. You listen better. You speak with less fear and more faith. This becomes the foundation of your child's growth.

Parent Perspective: *"I always thought my son was lazy. Every time I asked him to do something, I already had frustration in my tone. Then one day he said, 'Why do you always act like I'm gonna mess up?' That's when it hit me. I wasn't giving him a chance to rise, I was assuming he'd fall."*

Make A No-Yelling Reset Plan

Yelling rarely comes out of the blue. It builds up quietly and then bursts out quickly. Your child left their winter coat at school, and it's below freezing. You've asked your child to turn off the TV for the third time, but they aren't listening. It doesn't take much. Suddenly, the voice you didn't want to use is the one echoing through your house.

You didn't intend to yell. You didn't wake up thinking, *"Today I'm going to lose it."* But here's the good news: if you can recognize the signs of yelling, you can stop it. That's what a reset plan is for.

A **reset plan** is your personal pattern breaker. It's not a rigid script or a perfect solution. It's a simple, practiced sequence you can use when everything feels overwhelming. Think of it like an emotional emergency brake—something you've rehearsed beforehand, so your body can reach for calm even when your mind feels chaotic.

How to Build Your Reset Plan?

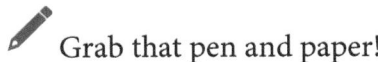 Grab that pen and paper!

Step 1: Know Your Red Flags

Yelling does not occur randomly. Your body detects it before you do. Take a moment to name your early warning signs:

- Jaw Clenching
- Voice getting sharp
- Tired but wired
- Feeling like you want to walk out or shut down

Complete this sentence:

"When I feel _____, I know I'm close to yelling."

Your feelings aren't your weaknesses. They're a sign that your system is raising a red flag and giving you a chance to pause before you reach the point of no return.

Step 2: Build Your Micro-Pause

A micro-pause isn't a self-inflicted time-out. It's a 10-second intervention.

Review and identify some of the items below that might relax your nervous system:

- Put your hand on your chest.
- Take 3 slow breaths.
- Walk to the sink and run cold water.
- Say, *"I need a second,"* and step out of the room.

It doesn't have to be pretty, but it should be **intentional.** The goal isn't calm. The goal is interruption.

Step 3: Use a Grounding Phrase

Have a line ready that grounds you. For example:

- *"This isn't an emergency."*
- *"This is hard, but I can handle it."*
- *"My calm is the lesson."*
- *"Breathe first. Then speak."*

Pick one, or write your own. Repeat it out loud or silently. Don't fake it; use words that work for you. Find your phrase to find your footing.

Step 4: Don't Just Recover, Reconnect

The reset phase isn't finished when you calm down. It's finished when you reconnect with your child. When you're ready, return to your child not just with instructions, but with presence.

Get on their level. Meet their eyes. Say something simple like:

- *"That was a lot. Let's try again."*
- *"I felt overwhelmed when I yelled at you, and I'm working on it."*
- *"I'm here. Let's do this together."*

Reconnecting doesn't mean you're letting your child off the hook. You're showing them what repair looks like. In this way, they learn that big feelings don't have to lead to big harm.

You'll yell sometimes. That's inevitable. However, when you take the time to create, internalize, and use your grounding phrase, you **catch your anger sooner, reset faster, and repair better.** One moment at a time.

Chapter 4 Recap:
The Calm Starts with You

1. **Your calmness is not a personality trait; it's a skill that you can develop.** It grows through self-awareness, nervous system regulation, and daily practice.

2. **Reacting is automatic. Responding is intentional.** The shift begins with noticing your triggers before they take over.

3. **"Just breathe" isn't enough.** Real regulation comes from sending safety signals to your body, not forcing stillness.

4. **Emotional regulation is contagious.** When you model it, your child learns how to deal with big feelings without fear.

5. **The self-fulfilling prophecy: What you expect, you create.** Kids tend to become who we believe they are. Your expectations shape tone, responses, and connections.

6. **A reset plan gives you a pause button.** Having a practiced sequence helps you gain calm before yelling takes over.

CHAPTER 5

SAY IT BETTER

"Speak to your children as if they are the wisest, kindest, most beautiful humans on Earth, for what they believe is what they will become." – Brooke Hampton

Power Struggles: Don't Take the Bait

Power struggles occur when two people try to control the same situation simultaneously. In that emotional tug-of-war, no one really wins. Everyone ends up feeling frustrated, unheard, or overwhelmed.

Picture this:

You say, "Time to get dressed." Your child replies, "I don't want to." You repeat, this time more firmly, "Get dressed now." Your child pushes back louder: "No! You can't make me!"

And just like that, it's no longer about getting dressed. It's about getting power.

Here's what's really happening beneath the surface: the moment shifts from connection to control. You're trying to assert your authority while your child is trying to assert their independence. Suddenly, you both feel stuck in a standoff that neither of you wanted.

Children don't resist testing your patience, but because they want to feel like they have an opinion in a world where most decisions are made for them. When they say "no," they're often really saying, *"I want to be my own person."*

And for parents? That resistance can poke at something sensitive fear of losing control, being disrespected, or raising a child who won't listen. Here's the shift: When you stay grounded and hold the boundary without raising your voice, you lead.

Parenting isn't about overpowering. It's about staying calm and clear when you speak to them, especially when things get loud. That's where the connection lies.

Hold The Line Without the Fight

So how do you avoid the power struggle without giving in? You hold the boundary, but you do it with calm, clarity, and connection.

Here's how that can look in real life:

- **Validate without surrendering:**

  <u>You say:</u> "You don't feel like getting dressed right now. That makes sense—your pajamas are cozy."

  <u>Why?</u> You're acknowledging their experience, not agreeing with the behavior. Validation doesn't equal permission—it just says, *I see you.*

- **Offer 2 good choices:**

  <u>You say:</u> "Do you want to wear the red shirt or the blue one? You choose."

  <u>Why?</u> This gives your child a sense of independence within boundaries. They don't get to skip getting dressed, but they *do* get to decide what to wear.

- **Hold the line gently:**

  <u>You say:</u> "Getting dressed isn't optional. I'll sit here with you while you decide."

  <u>Why?</u> You're not backing down. However, you're not powering up either. You're showing your child that *we can stay connected even when we disagree.*

Parent Perspective: *"I used to think if I didn't 'win,' I'd lose authority. But the less I fight, the more my kids cooperate. Not because I give in but because I stay calm."*

You're not forfeiting control by staying calm. You're showing what healthy control looks like. Let them have the small wins—such as choosing the shirt color, a snack plate, and the steps in the bedtime routine. Save your strength for what matters the most: Safety, respect, and connection.

You don't need to "win" in the moment. You just need to **lead** it.

POWER STRUGGLE   OFFER 2 GOOD CHOICES

How Listening Becomes Your Superpower

When your child is upset, it's natural to want to jump in, explain, fix, or talk them out of whatever they're feeling. You want to make it better. You want to calm things down. But here's the truth: often what your child really needs isn't a solution; they need your full attention.

They don't need a speech. They don't need a fast fix. They need to feel like you're truly with them—really present. Not with half an ear while making dinner, not with a quick "uh-huh" while scrolling your phone, but with true presence. Real, grounded, eye-to-eye, heart-to-heart presence.

For a child, being truly heard is a regulating experience. It's what calms their nervous system. It's what tells them: You matter. You make sense. I'm still here with you even in the hard moments.

Sometimes the most powerful thing you can say is nothing at all. Just your quiet, steady listening is enough to help them come back to the center. To understand your child well, you must listen attentively. It sounds simple, but it's not easy. Then again, most things that are worthwhile aren't easily achieved. Understanding begins with listening.

Connect By Listening

Children don't always have the words to explain what's going on inside them. Instead, they express their emotions through behavior: whining, slamming doors, shouting things like "You *never listen!*" or "*I hate you!*" It's raw. It's loud. It's messy. But it's still communication, and you need to listen to them. Listening doesn't mean you agree to whatever they say. It means you're tuning in with curiosity instead of criticism. It's saying, *"You don't have to yell to be heard."*

Try making these small but powerful shifts:

These language tweaks might seem like subtle changes, but they have a big, positive impact. They move you from correction to connection. Connection is what softens defenses and invites calm.

Research shows that active listening lowers defiance, increases cooperation, and builds secure attachment—especially in moments of emotional distress. The next time your child comes to you with big emotions, remember: **you don't have to fix it. You just have to listen to it.** Listening is more than a skill. It's your superpower.

Here's what this can look like in reality:

Parent Perspective: "*My 5-year-old screamed that I was the 'worst daddy ever' after I said no to more screen time. I wanted to snap back. Instead, I moved down to his level and said, 'Whoa, that felt really big to you, huh?' He just burst into tears and said, 'I just wanted one more show.' We talked. He calmed down. I didn't yell. That was new for both of us.*"

That's the power of listening. When you look past the outburst and truly listen to what your child is trying to communicate, they feel heard. **When your child feels understood, they don't scream.**

How To Practice Listening

- **Pause, don't react.** Stay grounded. Relax your shoulders. Let a long exhale release some of the tension.

- **Reflect on what you hear, then respond.** Try: "*You're upset because I said no.*"

    Or: "*You wish things felt fairer.*"

- **Don't rush to fix.** Allow the feeling to exist. Sit with it for a moment, even if it's uncomfortable.

- **Use your body to connect.** Nod. Make eye contact. Sit at their level.

A child who feels seen is more likely to listen. And listening isn't just something you do; it's something you model. When your child feels heard, they feel safe. When they feel safe, their defenses drop, and real connection can begin.

Why Does Non-Verbal Communication Matter?

Before your child hears you say a single word, they've already read your face, posture, and tone.

We often focus on *what* to say when we want our kids to listen, rather than on how we deliver those words and our accompanying body language. Non-verbal communication is heard first and the loudest.

Think about it: If you say, "*I'm not mad*," but your jaw is tight, your voice is sharp, and your arms are crossed, what will your child believe? Body language always tells the truth.

This is especially true for young children. Their developing brains don't just listen to words; they track physical cues. Your tone, expression, and posture can convey more to them than your words do. To them, your voice is your message.

So, when you say, "*You're safe*," but your body says, "*I'm about to snap*," your child senses the mismatch. That disconnect can make them anxious and can even escalate their misbehavior. Because their nervous system is trying to make sense of something that doesn't feel safe.

Speak With Your Body. Here's How:

- Soften your face before speaking. Take a slow breath. Unclench your jaw. Drop your shoulders.

- Get to their eye level; it helps regulate both of you.
- Speak slowly. Not because you feel calm, but because you're choosing calm.
- Use fewer words. Let your presence do the work.
- Keep your hands and arms open—not pointed, clenched, or crossed.

Parent Perspective: *"The moment I stopped standing over my son and sat down next to him, everything changed. I didn't even say anything different. I just stopped hovering. I started being with him instead of talking at him."*

You don't have to say it perfectly. You just have to *say it* with conviction. Not louder—just slower. Not harsher, but warmer. Not forcefully, but clearly. When your presence says, *"I'm here. I care. I'm trying,"* your child doesn't just hear you; they feel you.

Empathy Comes First

We often think of empathy—the ability to understand and share someone else's feelings—as something we're supposed to teach our kids. However, here's the truth: empathy can't be taught like a lesson, it starts as a gift. As their parent, you're the first person to give it to them. How? By showing it, especially when your child is having a hard time.

When your child feels seen and understood, their defenses soften. What might have been a battle earlier becomes a moment of connection. Empathy is the bridge that connects their messy moment to your calm presence. It transforms resistance into receptiveness not by force, but through emotional safety.

Let's take it a step further: Empathy isn't saying, *"It's okay that you hit your brother."* It's saying, *"You were really upset. I'm here to help you handle that feeling in a way that doesn't hurt anyone."*

It's critical to remember that showing empathy doesn't mean letting things slide. It doesn't mean ignoring the behavior. It means starting from this place: *"Your feelings make sense. You make sense. Now let's figure out what to do with all of this."*

This shift changes everything.

Instead of saying: *"Stop crying. It's not a big deal."*

Try: *"That felt really upsetting, huh? Want to tell me about it?"*

See the difference? You're not minimizing. You're not fixing. You're simply holding space, and that's powerful.

Empathy In Action

When kids feel misunderstood, criticized, or judged, their defenses rise. You'll recognize it in the form of yelling, shutting down, eye rolls, or non-cooperation. They're not necessarily being defiant when they display these behaviors. Rather, they're protecting themselves emotionally.

Here's the shift: When your child feels emotionally safe—that someone is *with* them, not *against* them—they start to let that armor down. That's when connection becomes possible.

Your child is incapable of thinking logically or reasoning during a heated moment unless they feel connected to you. Their brain can't process correction until their nervous system feels calm enough to receive it. That's why empathy always comes before correction.

Now you might be thinking, *"But I don't want to reward bad behavior with softness."* That's a valid concern many parents share.

So, let's make the distinction clear: Empathy doesn't excuse unwanted behavior, but showing it helps your child feel safe enough to learn why their behavior is unwanted.

Empathy addresses the *feeling* behind the behavior. Discipline addresses the *behavior*. We can, and must, show empathy while maintaining discipline. However, they have to be in that order.

So, when your child slams a door because you said no, try responding with something along these lines: *"That was loud. You didn't like my answer. I'm still here, and I love you."*

Once calm returns and they're receptive to what you have to say, you can address the boundary: *"In our home, we don't slam doors when we're upset. Let's talk about another way to handle big feelings next time."*

Be Curious, Not Furious

Parent Perspective: *"My son threw his cereal bowl across the kitchen when I said screen time was over. I was about to yell—I mean, cereal got scattered everywhere. But something in me told me to pause. I knelt and said, 'That looked like a big feeling. Did your body just explode with frustration?' His lip quivered, and he said, "All I wanted was to finish Ninjago." In that moment, everything shifted. He didn't* *need a consequence. He needed to know that I saw him, and his feelings made sense, even if his actions didn't."*

Empathy isn't about fixing the problem right away; it's about meeting your child in the moment, right where they are. Remember: It's the bridge between emotional chaos and calm connection. As this parent's story shows, sometimes the biggest shift happens when we respond to the feeling, not just the behavior.

Here are a few simple, powerful ways to practice empathy in the heat of everyday moments:

- Mirror your child's emotions verbally: *"You're really frustrated right now."*
- Get curious instead of furious: *"Something must've felt really hard for you."*
- Stay with the feeling before solving the problem.
- Speak slowly and lower your voice; a calming tone communicates safety.

Why does all this matter so much? According to the Gottman Institute, an organization committed to fostering and sustaining healthy relationships, when parents respond with empathy, children develop:

- Better emotional regulation
- Stronger parent-child bonds
- Higher emotional intelligence

Empathy isn't permissive parenting. Empathy is parenting with presence. It's not saying *"Yes"* to the behavior. It's saying *"Yes"* to the human underneath it.

When kids feel emotionally understood, they don't need to fight for control. They trust that they're safe even when they're struggling. And that trust? That's where real cooperation begins.

Powerful Alternatives to Yelling: Dos and Don'ts

Here are 5 of the most common habits that lead to yelling, and what to do instead:

- **DON'T REPEAT—MIX THINGS UP**

Repeating yourself multiple times- *"Put on your shoes. Come on, shoes. I said, shoes!"*—might feel like parenting to you, but to a child, it often sends a different message: *You don't really have to listen the first time.* Kids start to learn that they don't need to act until your voice gets louder or sharper. It unintentionally trains them to wait for the escalation.

Instead, shift your approach. If your child isn't responding, don't stay across the room repeating yourself. Walk over. Gently touch their shoulder. Get down on their level. Say it once, calmly and clearly, while making eye contact:

"Hey, it's time to put on your shoes now. I'll help you if you need it."

That small shift—lesser volume, more presence speaks louder than any raised voice.

- ## KEEP IT SIMPLE

"Get your shoes, brush your teeth, clean up your toys, and meet me at the door in five minutes." To you, that might sound like an efficient list. To your child? It's overwhelming. Too many instructions at once can trigger stress or an all-out shutdown, especially in younger children or those who are already easily distracted or need additional emotional support.

Instead, try this: *"Let's start with shoes. I'll help."* Once that's done, move to the next step.

Parent Perspective: *"I used to run through the full morning routine like a checklist and then wonder why my son just stood there. Now I say, 'Let's start with socks,' and suddenly, we're moving."*

Short, clear directions reduce confusion, prevent pushback, and help your child succeed—one step at a time.

- ## DON'T COMMAND, INVITE

Kids are more likely to resist when they feel like they've been bossed around all day. Commands like *"Do this"* or *"Stop that"* can put them in a defensive mode, especially when tension is already high.

Some situations that call for clear direction—*"Go brush your teeth now"*—aren't wrong. However, when the moment allows, try softening your tone to invite cooperation instead of triggering resistance.

Instead of, *"Pick that up now,"* try, *"Let's clean this part together—I'll do the books, you grab the blocks."*

Or ask, *"Do you want to put your pajamas on first, or brush your teeth first?"*

Using *"let's"* instead of *"you,"* or offering a small choice, can shift the mood from conflict to teamwork.

- ## DON'T THREATEN, STAY GROUNDED

"If you don't clean this up, no TV for a week!"

Sounds familiar? Threats can feel powerful in the moment—like you're finally getting control. But they usually backfire. Either the consequence is too extreme to enforce, or it creates a power struggle that pushes your child further away.

Instead of threatening, hold the boundary calmly and clearly: "You chose not to clean up, so you can't play with these toys for a little while." No anger. No drama. Just cause and effect.

Parent Perspective: *"When I stopped threatening and just followed through once or twice without yelling, everything changed. My son stopped testing me for every little thing because I wasn't reacting; I was responding."*

Maintain the boundaries with **neutral** tone and body language. Not as a punishment for the sake of correcting, but as a response to their choice.

- ## BE THE GROWN-UP

Your child yells, slams the door in your face. It stings. And if you've had a long day, it can feel deeply personal. But moments like this aren't about you, they're about a child who doesn't yet know how to manage big emotions, like frustration. They're testing your boundaries, not your worth.

What is the best thing you can do? Stay steady. Respond with something like: *"I won't let you talk to me that way. I'm here when you're ready to speak respectfully."*

You don't need to yell back or prove your authority. Your calm presence silently teaches them how to return to their own sense of calm. Kids feel safest when we don't match their chaos but anchor it.

Chapter 5 Recap:

Say it Better

1. Power struggles fade when you **lead with calm, not control**.

2. **Listening intently builds more trust** than lectures.

3. **Your tone and body language matter more than your words.**

4. **Clear, simple directions** help kids follow through.

5. An **"empathy-first"** approach in parenting opens the door to real cooperation and communication between you and your child.

CHAPTER 6

WHY SELF-CARE

"You can't pour from an empty cup. Take care of yourself first."
– Unknown

Put on Your Oxygen Mask First

You've likely heard this phrase a hundred times: "*Put on your oxygen mask first.*" It's a metaphor that reminds you to take care of yourself before tending to others. However, it isn't just a catchy metaphor. It's a survival strategy. When a plane loses cabin pressure, oxygen masks drop down because without oxygen, people may pass out. If you, as a parent, pass out, you can't help your child. In parenting, your oxygen isn't air, it's regulation. It's having a full tank. It's having enough emotional bandwidth to handle the spills, sass, and the 7th "*Mom!*" in a row without losing your cool.

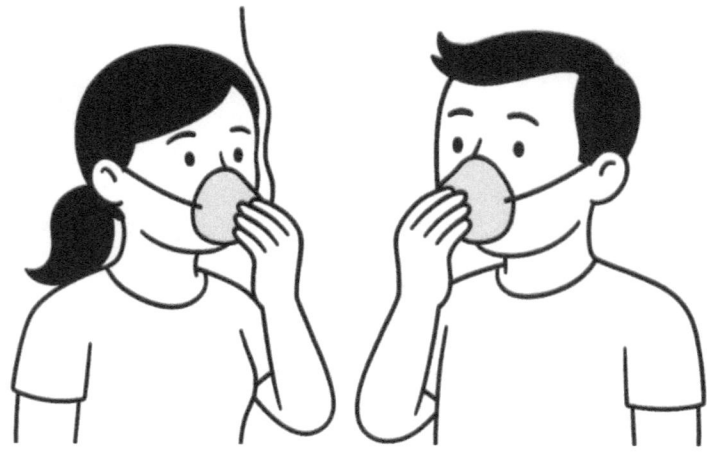

You can't parent from depletion.

In reality, when you're deep in the trenches of parenting—when the laundry is piled up high, when you forgot to pick up cookies for your 10-year-old's holiday party, or the 5-year-old wants brownies for dinner—the idea of pausing for *anything* that resembles self-care can feel laughable. *"Sure, let me just roll out my yoga mat while the house burns down around me."*

Many of us were taught that being a "good parent" means sacrificing ourselves for our children—loving your child means giving *everything* until there's nothing left for you. So, we keep pushing, even when we're exhausted. Even when our bodies are screaming for rest or support. We keep going because that's what we believe good parents do. And then we snap. Not because we're failing, but because our tank is empty.

The Snap Isn't About the Spill

When you snap at your child for asking a simple question, or you yell over something trivial, it doesn't mean you're a monster; it means you're a human. A human that's stretched thin—possibly for days, weeks, or longer. You're trying to parent without oxygen.

Parent Perspective: *"I realized I hadn't had a quiet moment to myself in 3 days. No wonder I screamed when my son spilled the milk. It wasn't the milk; it was everything I hadn't paused to feel."*

Self-care doesn't mean that you're living a life of luxury. It's not about spa days or "me time" that feels impossible to find. It's about moments, micro-breaks, little ways to refill before you run out. Here are some examples of actions to take when you're empty:

- Step outside for five minutes of quiet.
- Let your partner take over bedtime while you breathe.
- Eat real food instead of finishing your kid's leftovers.
- Look in a mirror and say this out loud: *"I matter too."*

When you take care of yourself, your energy, and your inner world, you don't just feel better. You show up better. You respond better. You parent better. You become the calm in the chaos. You recover faster after you lose it, and you teach your child what it looks like to value your own needs and theirs.

So go ahead and put on your oxygen mask first. Not because you matter more than your child, but because your calm helps them breathe, too.

Why Tired Looks Like Angry

You're not snapping because you're impatient. You're not yelling because you're a bad parent. You're shutting down because you're depleted. Not lazy. Not dramatic. Just worn out—physically, emotionally, and mentally. It's not the milk spill that sets you off; it's the mental state you're in when it happens.

When we're overtired, even a spilled drop of juice feels like a disaster. Something that wouldn't faze you on a good day feels impossible to handle the next moment.

You're not just sleepy—you're *tired in your bones.* You feel drained even after a long nap or a good night's sleep. Why? Because you're experiencing emotional exhaustion—the kind that builds from being "on" all the time. Answering one million questions, mediating sibling fights, or making nonstop decisions.

How to Hold it Together When You Feel Like Falling Apart

On the outside, you put up a strong front and keep going like you're fine. You feel like you have to be fine. But underneath, there's a quiet buildup. You might be able to hide it from your partner, child, coworkers, and friends, but your body and brain can't be tricked.

How Does Exhaustion Affect Your Brain

Here's what most people don't realize: When you're worn out, your brain changes the way it operates. Your prefrontal cortex, responsible for logic, empathy, and self-control, starts to shut down. The part of your brain wired for survival, the amygdala, steps in instead.

That's why you can go from calm to snapping in seconds. The logical, thoughtful part of your mind is offline. What's left is pure reaction—no filter, no pause button.

Parent Perspective: *"I had no idea how different I was when I was sleep-deprived. The mess, the noise, even how my daughter chewed her food—it all felt like a personal attack."*

That's what exhaustion does. It turns everyday life into a threat. The whining sounds like a fire alarm. The half-finished homework feels like a personal affront. You're overreacting because your nervous system is overstimulating.

But here's the good news: You can guide your brain back to calm. Sometimes the best reset isn't a tool or a phrase; it's a nap. Or it's stepping outside for 60 seconds. Or placing your hand on your chest and saying, *"I'm okay."* Even the smallest moment of pause tells your body and brain: *"You're safe. You can come down now."*

Why Small Things Can Feel So Big

Let's dig a little deep into another kind of tiredness: **Decision fatigue.**

Research shows that decision fatigue can impair your ability to think clearly, remain calm, and regulate emotions—essential skills for effective parenting. If you've ever wondered why your patience seems to vanish at bedtime, why the dinner table feels like a battleground, and why you're snapping over something trivial, it's because you're experiencing decision fatigue.

Each task, thought, and decision you make throughout the day may appear small on its own. But collectively, they wear down your mental capacity. It's like your brain is carrying a backpack that gets a little heavier with every decision you make. If you've ever felt overwhelmed by something as simple as "What's for dinner?" that's a classic sign of decision fatigue.

You may not realize it, but as a parent, you make dozens or even hundreds of decisions a day. Some are tiny. Some are huge. Some you make on autopilot. Some decisions are made while you're making a doctor's appointment, answering a work email, or managing a meltdown. And every single one takes effort.

Now add **emotional labor** on top of all those decisions. Emotional labor is the invisible work of anticipating everyone's needs, managing their emotions, and keeping the household running smoothly. It's no wonder that by 6:00 p.m., your brain feels fried. You're overloaded.

Parent Perspective: *"By the time I've answered 47 questions, planned meals, helped with homework, and remembered to RSVP to a birthday party, I have zero bandwidth left. My kids start whining, and I'm yelling before I even realize it."*

This is what emotional labor feels like. No drama. Just relentless. It's the kind of tiredness that sits beneath the surface, always there, even on the good days.

Here's where it gets tricky: Emotional labor and decision fatigue don't always present themselves as exhaustion. Sometimes they look like irritation, zoning out, or losing patience with something trivial. You might think or say, *"I don't care anymore. Just do whatever."*

It's not that you don't care; it's that you've run out of capacity to manage one more thing. This is the kind of exhaustion that turns "Can you brush your teeth?" into a snap that you instantly regret.

Simple Actions You Can Take to Lighten Your Load

To prevent decision fatigue, you need to lighten your load first. By implementing some small changes, you can reduce mental load before it spills over into frustration or burnout.

Below are some proactive actions you can take to reduce that never-ending list of "to dos." Pick up a pen and paper. Make your own list of actions that resonate with you and refer to it when you feel overwhelmed.

- **Create simple routines.** A Monday–Wednesday–Friday breakfast schedule (e.g., eggs and toast on Monday, cereal and fruit on Wednesday, and so on) means fewer daily choices and fewer moments of standing in front of the fridge and wondering what to make.

- **Make a "what to say when" cheat sheet.** Write 2–3 go-to responses for common challenges (e.g., whining, refusing to listen, etc.). This way, in the heat of the moment, you won't have to think—you'll already have the words.

- **Say no to extra stuff.** You don't need to sign up for every field trip or volunteering you're asked to. Protecting your peace is a valid reason to opt out—no explanation needed.

- **Delegate decisions.** Let your 9-year-old decide which movie to watch for movie night. Allow your partner to prepare dinner a certain number of nights each week. You can't control everything, and it's ok to share the load.

These aren't just time-savers. They're sanity savers. When your mind is less cluttered, your heart has more space to show up with the calm, connected presence your child needs.

You're not overwhelmed because you're disorganized or doing it wrong. You're overwhelmed because you're carrying too much, making too many decisions, and thinking and feeling too much all at once.

It's not about working harder. It's about carrying less. Lighten the load. Make more space. You might just find yourself yelling less because you're finally supported.

Quick Recharge Habits for Busy Parents

You probably don't have an hour to yourself. You may not even have 10 minutes. And some days, even 2 minutes feels like a stretch.

But what if I told you that just 30 seconds could make a difference? In this section, you'll learn about the power of micro-recharge moments—tiny, intentional habits that calm your nervous system and reset your emotional state *before* the yelling starts—and how to incorporate them into your own life.

These aren't magical fixes. They won't solve every problem. But they're practical actions that shift you from reactive to proactive, as we covered in Part 1.

Tiny Habits, Big Shifts

What follows are fast, effective ways to reset your nervous system. Over time, what starts out as a conscious effort becomes a healthy habit.

1. RESET WITH ONE SONG

Pick one song that calms you. Just one. Play it during the morning chaos, after a hard conversation, or sing it to yourself while your child is in the middle of a meltdown in the next room. The song becomes your cue—a signal to pause, breathe, and reconnect with yourself. Don't multitask. Just breathe and listen.

Music activates your parasympathetic nervous system—the "rest and digest" mode—that signals your body: *You're safe; you can slow down.*

This 30-second pause might not change your child's behavior, but it *will* change how you respond to them.

2. WATER AND ICE

Hold an ice cube. Splash your face with cold water. Press something cool to the back of your neck. It sounds silly, but it works.

Cold stimulation can interrupt your brain's stress signals and trigger a calming response. It's a quick way to help your body reset itself.

Use cold stimulation, not just to cool off physically, but to re-center emotionally. Even 10 seconds of this can help shift you from overwhelmed to calm.

3. THE 4-4-4-4 BREATH (BOX BREATHING)

Inhale for 4 seconds.

Hold for 4 seconds.

Exhale for 4 seconds.

Hold for 4 seconds.

Repeat this thrice. It takes less than a minute. Do it in the bathroom. Do it with your eyes closed, your hand on your chest, or while you're scrolling on your phone: Whatever works. No one, but your body, needs to know. Your body will thank you.

This technique helps to slow your heart rate and sends signals of safety to your brain. It tells your nervous system, *"We're okay. We're coming back to calm."*

4. HAND OVER HEART

Place your hand on your chest. Feel the warmth. Take a breath in and say, *"I'm doing the best I can."*

It may seem small, but this simple act of self-soothing sends a powerful signal to your nervous system. It stimulates the vagal nerve, an important but not a commonly known nerve that runs through your body, carrying signals between your brain, heart, and digestive system. Activating this nerve helps shift you from fight-or-flight mode into a more grounded and regulated state.

When you activate the vagal nerve, you're showing yourself compassion and giving yourself a moment of love and care. When you can hold yourself with compassion, you're more able to hold your child through their hard moments, too.

5. Laugh On Purpose

Watch a short video that makes you laugh. Send a meme to a friend. Scroll to that one clip that always feels funny. Humor is a circuit breaker—it helps to de-stress in a healthy way.

Parent Perspective: *"I keep a folder of funny videos on my phone for days I want to scream. I didn't realize how powerful it could be to just... laugh."*

Laughter releases feel-good hormones, relieves your tension, and brings you back to peace.

You don't have to put all the actions into practice all at once. Start by trying any one. Practice it for a week, then try for another week.

Sometimes, what you need the most isn't discipline or strategy. You just need a good laugh to find your way back to yourself. And every time you choose regulation over reaction, you're not just helping yourself—you're shaping how your child learns to handle their hard moments, too.

Love Yourself, Love Your Kids

Let's start with something that might feel uncomfortable:

Taking care of yourself isn't separate from loving your kids; it *is*, in fact, loving your kids.

Many parents carry quiet guilt when they rest. When they say 'no.' When they take time for themselves. There's that nagging voice: *Shouldn't you be doing more? Shouldn't you be giving more?*

You might not be hearing this enough: **You're not abandoning your child by resting. You're giving them access to the parent they need.**

Self-care isn't indulgent. It's not selfish. It's not just about bubble baths or spa days. It's about tending to your own emotional, physical, and mental well-being so that you aren't parenting from a place of depletion.

Parent Perspective: *"I thought being a good mom meant putting myself last. But I was always yelling. The first time I chose to rest instead of cleaning the mess, I felt guilty. But later that day, my son curled up next to me. I laughed. I didn't snap. I felt like myself again."*

That moment wasn't just about rest—it was about reconnecting with herself. This is what self-care does to you. It lets you:

- **Recharge** your patience.
- **Rebuild** your emotional capacity.
- **Reconnec**t with who you are beyond being someone's parent.

Self-care isn't indulgence. It's maintenance. It says, *"I matter, too."* When your needs are met, you don't just survive parenthood, you show up for it with more of yourself, and that's what your child needs the most.

And Your Child Notices.

When you pause to reset, your child learn that taking a rest isn't something you earn through burnout. When you set a boundary, they learn it's not about disconnecting, it's about self-respect. When you maintain your boundaries with compassion, they learn their boundaries are normal, too.

Research by Dr. Kristin Neff (University of Texas at Austin) and Dr. Laura Markham (Founder of Aha! Parenting and trained at Columbia University) shows that self-compassion in parents is associated with lower stress levels, improved emotional regulation, and a stronger parent-child connection.

In other words, your self-care isn't something extra—it's **essential.** Let it be the foundation of your parenting, not just a backup plan. Tell yourself, as often as you need:

"I'm not a better parent when I ignore my needs. I'm a better parent when I honor them."

Chapter 6 Recap:

Why Self-Care?

1. **When you yell at your child, you might feel like a failure, which is far from the truth.** There's a good chance you're feeling and responding to emotional fatigue.

2. **Avoid burnout.** When you're burned out, it's harder to stay calm.

3. **Small resets**, like taking a long breath or a small break, make a big difference.

4. **Taking care of yourself helps you parent with more patience and connection**, while having the added benefit of quietly modeling this behavior for your child.

5. **Self-care is essential** for peaceful and present parenting.

Understanding Your Child

Part III

CHAPTER 7

WHAT'S BEHIND YOUR CHILD'S BEHAVIOR?

"When little people are overwhelmed by big emotions, it's our job to share our calm, not join their chaos." – L.R. Knost

Misbehavior is Miscommunication

You're standing in the kitchen. Your child is melting down again. Maybe it's the wrong cup. Or the sandwich that you cut into pieces when they wanted it whole. Or you asked them to pause the iPad. Your brain spirals: *Why are they acting like this? What did I do wrong?*

It's easy to take misbehavior personally, to see it as defiance or a reflection of your parenting. Misbehavior is not about your child being "bad," and it's not about you failing as a parent. Misbehavior is miscommunication. It often happens because it's the easiest way for your child to say, "Something's not right. I need help."

Adults do this, too. When you're upset with your partner or a close friend, you might go quiet. You might slam the cabinet or sigh loudly. You're not trying to be dramatic; you're trying to be seen. You're communicating your internal state without words. Kids do the same thing, just more often and in more obvious ways.

Unlike adults, children lack the emotional language or regulation skills to express what they're feeling. So, instead of saying, "I feel overwhelmed," they scream. Instead of saying, "I need attention," they whine, or hit, or say something rude. Their behavior signals something deeper inside them.

Parent Perspective: *I used to think my daughter's defiance was just her testing my limits. But when I paused and really listened to her, I realized she was trying to tell me, 'I don't feel heard.' Acknowledging her misbehavior as a form of communication instead of rebellion changed everything for us.*

When you respond with curiosity instead of criticism, you teach your child: "You don't have to act out to be heard. I'll listen before the screaming starts."

That doesn't mean there aren't consequences. It means responding from a place of connection, not control. The real goal isn't just stopping the behavior; it's understanding what drives it.

The Hidden Messages Behind the Misbehavior

Every negative behavior has a reason. Your child might act out to get attention, escape an uncomfortable task, satisfy a sensory need, or express a feeling they can't yet name.

Some kids melt down when they're hungry, scared, or tired. Others might act out when they feel unsafe or out of control. One child might kick because that's the only thing they *can* control. Another might pull at clothes simply for the sensory input. A child who's repeatedly been ignored might shout louder—not because they want to be difficult, but because they're using behavior to send a message that words haven't been able to get across. Once we understand that, we stop asking, *"What's wrong with them?"* and start wondering, *"What's happening to them?"*

Try this mental shift. Instead of:

- "They're being bad." Say: "They're having a hard time."
- "They're trying to push my buttons." Say: "They're trying to feel some control."
- "They're just doing this to get attention." Say: "They need connection."

Excusing, allowing, or ignoring your child when they act out isn't the solution. Instead, try to understand what's going on beneath the surface. When you take an approach that leads with curiosity instead of control, your child might stop feeling like a problem to fix and start feeling like a person to support.

Don't Miss the Teachable Moment

You may feel an urgent need to respond to your child's misbehavior instead of taking a measured approach. Often, these situations lend themselves to **teachable moments** instead of harsh responses.

Parents are teachers of life. You teach your child how to manage frustration, repair a relationship, and ask for what they need. You can't teach effectively when you are angry. And your child can't learn when they are angry.

The next time a difficult moment arises, ask yourself:

- *Did I teach something just now?*
- *Or did I just react?*
- *Will they remember the message, or just the tone of my voice?*

Parent Perspective: *After yelling at my son for talking back, I realized I had no idea what he actually needed. I just wanted his behavior to stop. Later, I asked him, "What were you trying to say when you said that?" His answer made me realize that he felt unheard, and it changed everything. We ended up talking about respect instead of a one-way conversation where I was demanding it.*

That's what a teachable moment does, but only if you recognize it at the right time. The next time your child's behavior triggers you, pause and ask yourself: **Is this a moment to punish, or a moment to teach?**

The lessons that shape your child the most often come *right after* their behavior you like the least.

Under Construction: Your Child's Brain

You know those moments when your child melts down because they can't figure out the zipper on their jacket, or scream like it's the end of the world when they can't find that Lego block? You think, *"Seriously? This is what we're doing right now?"*

It's okay to feel baffled. However, understanding one simple truth can change how you see these moments: **Your child's brain is still under construction.**

Your child's brain isn't fully developed yet, and that's not a flaw. It's just biology. The emotional center of their brain is fully active from birth. However, the part of the brain that manages logic, empathy, impulse control, and problem-solving is still developing, and it takes decades to mature fully. This is why your 5-year-old can memorize dinosaur facts but can't remember to put on their shoes. It's not because they're defiant. It's because their brain is still learning how to manage stress.

The Upstairs and Downstairs Brain

Dr. Dan Siegel, a clinical professor of psychiatry at the UCLA School of Medicine and executive director of the Mindsight Institute, along with Dr. Tina Payne Bryson, uses the powerful metaphor of the *"upstairs brain"* and *"downstairs brain."*

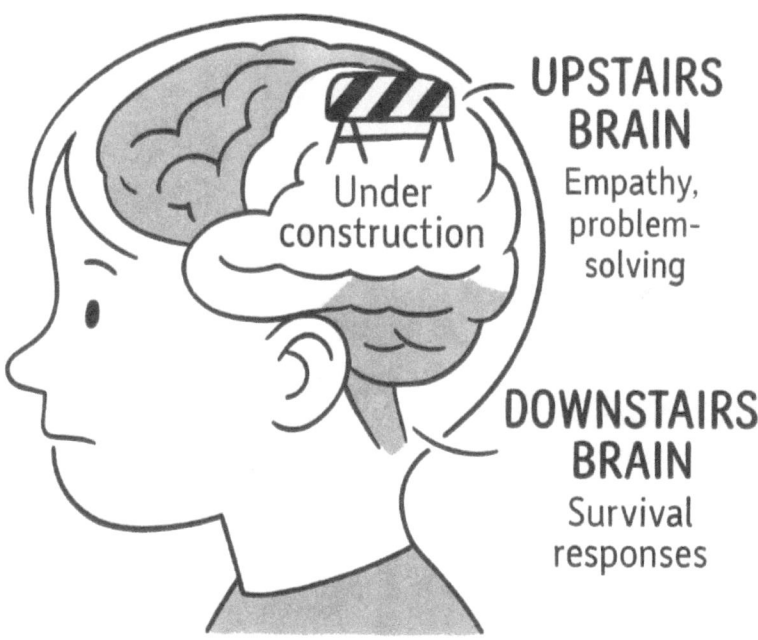

- **The downstairs brain** controls survival responses like fight, flight, and freeze. It's primitive and reactive. Think of it as the emotional engine, ready to protect but not particularly adept at logical thinking.

- **The upstairs brain** is responsible for empathy, reflection, and problem-solving. This part of the brain is still under construction, and it will be fully developed in your child's twenties.

When your child is overwhelmed and starts yelling, hitting, or storming off, that's their downstairs brain taking over. They aren't "choosing" chaos. They're having a hard time coping.

Knowing Better Isn't the Same as Doing Better

Even if your child knows the rule, that doesn't mean they can follow it consistently, especially when they're under stress. Adults lose it sometimes, too, even though we know better. So, the real question isn't, *"Why are they doing this again?"* but rather, *"What's getting in the way of them doing better?"*

The next time your child's upstairs brain takes over, ask yourself: Is this defiance or something else? Perhaps it's a skill gap, a stress response, a cry for connection, or something entirely different.

Putting this perspective into practice helps you to stop seeing their behavior as manipulation and start seeing it as communication. Often, your child isn't trying to give you a hard time. *They're* having a hard time. Misbehavior is their way of saying, *"Something's off. I need help."*

Relationship Strain? Train The Brain.

Children's brains aren't just shaped by what they learn; they're shaped by how they feel. The safer, more loving, and more predictable their environment feels to them, the stronger their neural pathways become for regulation and resilience. In other words, your presence doesn't just comfort your child; it builds their brain.

Neuroscience shows that repeated emotional experiences—such as being soothed after a meltdown or being heard in the middle of a frustrating moment—wire the brain for calmness, connection, and problem-solving. Neural pathways that are frequently used are strengthened, while the unused ones fade with time.

When you calmly say, *"You're really upset. I'm here,"* you're not spoiling your child. You're helping them build the circuit in their brain that will allow them to manage those emotions in the future.

What's Actually Age-Appropriate?

Have you ever thought, *"They should know better by now,"* or *"Why do I have to say the same thing a thousand times?"* Most of us carry invisible expectations and quiet assumptions about what our kids *should* be able to do. However, often, those expectations don't match what our child's brain and body are capable of.

You're not failing. Parenting feels ten times harder when we expect more from our kids than what they are developmentally capable of doing.

Here's what's most important to remember:

Growth Isn't a Straight Line

There's a common myth that kids should grow in neat, upward steps. However, in reality, childhood development is a complex and messy situation. It loops, stalls, leaps ahead, and circles back. One day, your child is sharing toys and saying "please." The next, they're yelling "Mine!" and throwing blocks across the room.

When they act like this, it doesn't mean that you've done something wrong; it means that their brain is still learning. Emotional growth requires a lot of repetition, followed by even more after that.

The next time you feel like your child should "know better," remember this: Regression isn't rebellion. It's part of the process. It's normal.

Expectation Check: What's Reasonable?

When we expect more from our child than they can developmentally handle, frustration builds on both sides. We feel like they're not trying hard enough, and they feel like they're never enough. The antidote is to match our expectations with their actual capacity—not just their age on paper, but their brain's stage of development.

Here's a helpful reframe:

> **Ages 2–4: Big feelings, tiny impulse control.**

Your child isn't throwing a tantrum because they're vying for a power play. They are genuinely emotionally overwhelmed. Your child may know one moment what they "should" do and do it flawlessly. Then, in the following month, when they're faced with a similar scenario, they completely fail. Consistency helps. But they may still need you to be their primary source of calm because they can't access theirs yet.

> **Ages 5–7: Emotions often outrun logic.**

They can follow more steps than those of the previous developmental stage—pause (sometimes) and reflect a little. But under stress—such as hunger, tiredness, sibling drama—they still fall apart quickly. They're not little adults yet. With your support, they're still practicing how to handle life's curveballs.

Remember, at this age, children may need you to repeat guidance multiple times. It's through repetition that they learn. Don't get frustrated, stay patient, and keep teaching.

> **Ages 8–10: They *can* think things through, but their stress regulation still wobbles.**

They begin to understand the concepts of fairness, social rules, and emotional consequences. But disappointment still stings hard. And just because they "knew better" doesn't mean they have the skills to do better in that moment.

> **Tweens & Teens: Sounding grown doesn't mean they feel grown.**

They crave independence and respect, but their emotions are intense, and their sense of identity is still developing. One moment, they want your advice. The next, they push you away. Beneath it all, they still need your steady presence.

Adjusting your expectations regarding your child's development doesn't mean you're lowering your standards. It means you're providing solid ground for them to stand on when they wobble. When you align your expectations with where your child stands rather than where you want them to be, you parent with more patience, and they grow with more confidence.

When Expectations Match Development, Everything Softens

This isn't about letting things slide. And it's not about lowering your standards.

Boundaries still matter, but now they're based on your child's actual abilities, not just your frustration over where you think they should be.

When your expectations align with your child's developmental pace, you yell less, empathize more, and your child stops feeling like a "problem" and starts feeling like a person in progress.

That's what builds real connection—not fear of consequences, but the **safety** of being understood. When a child feels truly understood, they're more likely to soften, try again, and grow.

Set Boundaries Early, Not Loudly

Setting boundaries can be confusing. You want to be firm, but not harsh. You want to be kind, but not permissive. When your child is melting down or pushing every button you have, you might feel like the only way to be heard is to shout. The most effective boundaries aren't set in the heat of the moment. They're set beforehand—early, calmly, and clearly. That's what makes them effective.

o Why Early Boundaries Matter

Think of boundaries like a seatbelt: You buckle it *before* the crash, not after. Setting boundaries early gives your child time to adjust, prepares their brain for transition, and prevents emotional distress. When you set boundaries, you convey to them, "You're safe because I'm leading." Waiting until things get chaotic to assert a limit often results in yelling—not because you're harsh, but because you're desperate.

Example: Instead of waiting until your child's jumping on the couch to yell, "Stop it right now!" you calmly say *before* they start to play, "We don't jump on the couch. If you feel jumpy, let's use the mat."

You're not waiting for the boundary to be broken—you're building it in advance.

○ Boundaries Build Safety

Imagine walking along a cliff without a railing. Even if you're careful, every step feels risky. Now imagine that same cliff with a sturdy fence. Suddenly, you can relax, breathe easier, and move with confidence.

That's what boundaries do to kids. They create structure, predictability, and trust. When a child pushes a limit (and they will), they're really asking: *Are you steady? Are you safe?* Boundaries that are created early and maintained consistently send a powerful message: *Yes. I've got you.*

Dr. Becky Kennedy, author of *Good Inside*, reminds us, "Our job is to keep our kids safe—physically and psychologically." Boundaries aren't about control. They're about care.

○ Boundaries in Action

Boundaries aren't about what you say, they're about what you *do*. Instead of saying, "Stop hitting your brother!" Try: "I won't let you hit your brother. If it continues, I'll need to move you away to keep everyone safe."

You're not threatening. You're following through.

You don't need to give a lecture. Your calm response, paired with steady presence, says it all. When your child tests your limit, they're not being manipulative. They're just checking: *Is this real? Can I trust you to hold it?*

Parent Perspective: *"Every time my daughter got overtired, bedtime turned into a screaming match. I realized we kept pushing the boundary later and later, and she didn't know where the line was. We* *scheduled the bedtime a little earlier and agreed in advance on what to expect. The meltdowns stopped almost overnight."*

That's the power of early boundaries—they prevent chaos by making the expectations clear *before* the overwhelm hits.

Building Boundaries with Empathy

Setting a boundary doesn't mean disconnecting from your child. In fact, the best boundaries are paired with emotional attunement. This approach is powerfully articulated by a renowned psychologist, Dr. John Gottman, whose research highlights the importance of 'emotion coaching.' Emotion coaching isn't about letting children do whatever they want; it's about acknowledging and validating their feelings first, while simultaneously guiding their behavior with clear boundaries.

This principle can be summarized as *'validate the mind, but control the actions,'* a core tenet of Gottman's approach that emphasizes understanding a child's emotional world while still guiding their behavior. This means we empathize with their emotions and help them understand what they're feeling, ensuring they feel seen and heard. Only then, from a place of connection, do we gently, yet firmly, direct their actions within established boundaries.

Try saying:

- ☺ *'I know it's hard to leave the park. We're going now. I'll hold your hand on the way.'* Here, you acknowledge their disappointment about returning home from the park, validating their feelings, before stating the boundary of going home.

☺ *'You're disappointed that I said no to the toy. I understand. That's a hard feeling.'* You're showing that you truly understand their internal experience, which builds connection and trust, even when the answer is 'no.'

☺ *'It's tough to stop video games when you get really into them. That's why we set a timer to help.'* By identifying with their difficulty, you're not dismissing their feelings, but rather reinforcing the structure that helps them manage those feelings.

You're not giving in, but you are parenting with empathy. That connection softens the boundary, so your child doesn't feel alone inside it.

Why Reasons Matter

Kids don't need long explanations. However, a simple and clear reason helps them understand the rationale behind the rule and increases their buy-in.

- 'We wear seatbelts to stay safe.'
- "We turn off screens before bed so your brain can rest."
- "We don't hit because you should treat others the way that you want to be treated."

Boundaries Are a Gift

Setting boundaries isn't about dominance; it's about leadership. You're helping your child feel safe, regulated, and understood. And you're doing it in a way that teaches rather than terrifies.

You don't have to yell. You don't have to wait until things fall apart. You can lead with clarity, empathy, and quiet confidence. And when you do, your child learns: *Limits are love. Boundaries are safety. I am held, not controlled.*

Setting the boundary doesn't mean that you're putting up a blockade. In fact, it's the opposite.

Chapter 7 Recap:

What's Behind Your Child's Behavior?

1. **Misbehavior or defiance is often a signal that your child needs emotional support.**

2. Kids act out because **their brains are still developing**.

3. **Meltdowns usually happen when kids feel safe** to release what they're feeling. When your child is overwhelmed, their downstairs brain—the part that responds to flight, fight, and freeze—takes over.

4. **When your expectations match your child's developmental stage, cooperation grows.**

5. **Set boundaries early and reinforce them often.** Doing so builds trust, safety, and long-term respect.

CHAPTER 8

REAL STRATEGIES FOR REAL CHALLENGES

"Discipline is not about punishment; it's about guidance."
– L.R. Knost

Understanding "Disrespect"

"Don't talk to me like that!"

"Excuse me? That tone is not okay."

"I can't believe you just rolled your eyes at me!"

Disrespect is one of the most triggering behaviors for many parents, not because they are too sensitive, but because it often hits something deep within them. It can stir up anger, defensiveness, and even hurt. Here's something important to remember: Most of the time when your child is disrespectful, it isn't actually about you. Many times, it's not personal at all; it's developmental.

Children often struggle to show respect, especially under stress. It's not that they're incapable; they're inexperienced. Respect is a learned skill, and like all other skills, it takes time, modeling, and repetition to master.

When your child slams objects, talks back, or rolls their eyes, it's not always a sign of rebellion. Often, this behavior is a sign of **dysregulation** and a lack of tools to express big feelings in respectful ways. Dysregulation is a concept that we've covered throughout this book in different forms.

Simply put, dysregulation is a state in which a child's emotional response is out of balance, often leading to a behavior that seems inappropriate or disproportionate. Recognizing this helps you guide your child rather than punish them, creating opportunities for their growth and understanding.

In moments like these, their rational, empathetic "upstairs brain" can go offline, allowing the reactive "downstairs brain" to take over. This isn't defiance, but a response to overwhelm.

A single conversation won't reinforce respect. Every eye roll or sarcastic tone is a chance to calmly guide them. No yelling, no shaming—just steady, clear teaching from a place of love. Just like you, your child can't change after one instance. They grow through what's modeled repeatedly.

When you understand this, you're more likely to respond with guidance rather than shame.

Let's look at a few reasons why your child might display disrespect:

1. **They don't know what respect looks like.** It's easy to say, *"Don't talk to me that way."* But have we modeled what it looks like to speak respectfully when frustrated? Kids need to be taught through example, not just correction.

2. **They're mirroring our behavior.** This is the hard one. Our children mimic our behavior. If we often respond with sarcasm, criticism, or dismissiveness, they may adopt that tone without us realizing it. Respect is a two-way street.

3. **There are no clear boundaries.** When disrespect is ignored or inconsistently addressed, kids don't learn what's acceptable. Boundaries teach our children what's okay and what's not with love and clarity, not anger and punishment.

4. **We're interpreting distress as defiance.** A slammed door might actually say, *"I'm overwhelmed."* A sarcastic tone might mask anxiety. When you pause and wonder, *"What's underneath this?"* you shift from policing behavior to supporting your child's emotional growth.

* A Note on Respect and Power

Respect doesn't emerge from fear. Respect comes from feeling seen. When kids are treated with dignity, especially when they're struggling, they learn to offer that same dignity in return.

Respect also isn't something children owe us automatically. It's something that grows in the soil of our relationship with them. When they feel respected by us, they're more likely to respect us back.

Ask yourself:

- Am I modeling the tone I want to hear?
- Am I staying consistent with boundaries?
- Am I interpreting their behavior as communication, not disrespect?

Bottom Line

All kids show disrespect from time to time, and it's always hard to deal with as a parent. It can push every button you have. But it's also an opportunity. When you shift from asking, "*Why are they treating me like this?*" to "*What are they trying to tell me?*" you open the door to growth, not just control.

And the transition from retaliation to regulation, from punishment to guidance, is what truly teaches your child the respect you're hoping for. You don't have to accept all behavior. But you *can* accept the child underneath it and guide them with patience, repetition, and love.

Everyday Challenges, Real Solutions

Now let's unpack what's really going on beneath the surface of common parenting stressors. Then you'll learn effective ways to handle them.

 Sibling Fights

You're in the kitchen and suddenly chaos comes barging in. There's screaming, grabbing, and someone yells, "That's mine!" and they're in tears. It's exhausting, and it can feel like you're failing. Sibling conflict isn't a sign that something's wrong. It's actually how kids learn emotional and social skills—if we help guide the process.

Sibling rivalry usually isn't about the toy, the couch cushion, or who got there first. It's about a deeper need.

"Do I matter as much as they do?"

"Can I still get attention when I need it?"

"Is there enough love, space, and power to go around?"

When kids feel emotionally out of sync—such as feeling overwhelmed, disconnected, or unseen—they act it out with the person closest to them, which is often a sibling.

✓ When to Step In (And When to Not)

Not every sibling argument needs your intervention. Kids benefit from practicing conflict resolution. However, if there's emotional or physical harm, or if the fight keeps escalating, that's your cue to step in as a guide, not as a judge.

✓ What Helps

- **Don't pick sides.** Focus on helping both kids feel heard rather than identifying who's "right."

- **Name the deeper need.** Try saying: *"Sounds like you both wanted time with that toy. Let's figure out a plan so you each get a turn."*

- **Remove the toy calmly.** *"The game's taking a break right now. We'll try again later."*

- **Model repair.** Let your kids hear you apologize and take responsibility for mistakes in your own relationships with friends, family, or your partner.

Sibling fights can be opportunities for lessons in boundaries, empathy, and emotional expression. You're not just managing the chaos; you're teaching your kids how to handle conflict and reconnect with each other.

☑ Lying

Your child says they brushed their teeth, but their toothpaste tube and toothbrush haven't moved since this morning. You feel frustrated and maybe even betrayed. You think, *"Why lie about something so trivial?"*

Remember: Most lying isn't about deception. It's about protection—trying to avoid shame, disapproval, or consequences. Lying is often a developmental coping mechanism, not a moral failure.

- **Younger kids** lie because their brains haven't fully developed the ability to hold two truths at once—"I did something wrong" and "I'm still a good person."

- **Older kids and teens** lie to protect their independence, avoid punishment, or manage anxiety about disappointing you.

- **Sensitive kids** lie because they fear conflict or rejection, even if the issue is small.

At its core, lying is often your child saying, *"I don't feel safe telling the truth right now."*

✓ What Helps

Instead of accusing your child for lying, shift to curiosity and connection. Try saying: "That doesn't quite add up. Want to try again? I'll stay calm." You're not excusing the lie—you're creating a safer space for honesty.

Other approaches:

- **Name the feeling underneath.** "It seems like you were worried I'd get mad if you told the truth."
- **Set the tone for honesty.** "In this house, mistakes are okay. But it's brave to be honest."
- **Avoid harsh punishment.** Fear makes kids better at lying, not honesty. Consequences for negative behavior can (and should) still happen, but you should lead with connection first.

When your child tells the truth—especially when it's hard—pause and acknowledge it:

"That was hard to say, but you told me the truth. That's courageous."

These moments not only build your child's character but also lay a foundation of trust. It will enable your child to keep coming to you when they get older or when the stakes are higher.

Scenario 1: Punitive Response

Dad: "You again?! What did you do now?"

Son: "No, Kevin pushed me!"

Dad: "You're always lying! You're nothing but a troublemaker."

This punitive response immediately instills fear in the child, leading them to use lying as a defense mechanism. The child learns that hiding or distorting the truth is safer to avoid parental anger. In the long run, this approach damages the parent-child trust, deprives the child of opportunities to acknowledge their mistakes and take responsibility, and hinders the development of problem-solving skills. If a child does not feel safe being honest, lying is likely to solidify into a recurring behavioral pattern.

Scenario 2: Understanding and Honesty-Focused Response

Dad: "Hey, tell me what happened."

Son: "Kevin did it! I didn't."

Dad: "In this house, mistakes are okay, but lying is not. Can you tell me the real story?"

Son: *(Hesitantly)* "I... I did it while I was playing with Kevin."

Dad: "Thank you for telling me that. It takes a lot of bravery to be honest. Next time, let's try to be more careful when you're playing."

This approach—emphasizing understanding and honesty—sends a clear message to the child: 'Mistakes are acceptable, but honesty is essential.' When parents show empathy and support instead of blame, the child feels safe enough to be vulnerable and tell the truth. This is crucial for helping children take responsibility for their actions, develop problem-solving skills, and build a deep trusting relationship with their parents. Through the positive experience of honesty, children can develop inner courage and a strong moral compass.

☑ Whining

Does the word *"pleeeaaaase"* said in a high-pitched, drawn-out voice makes your skin crawl? *Join the club!* Whining is one of the most universally triggering behaviors for parents. It's grating. It's persistent. And it often shows up at the worst moments—right before dinner, during transitions, or when you're already overwhelmed.

Here's a reframe that can shift everything: Whining isn't about manipulation. It's a signal of dysregulation.

✓ Why Kids Whine

Whining often occurs when a child's internal resources are running low. They may be:

- Hungry, tired, or overstimulated.
- Struggling to manage disappointment or delay.

- Unsure of how to ask for something in a calm, clear way.
- Testing whether whining will get a quicker result than using their "strong voice."

They aren't trying to be annoying (well, maybe sometimes they are). They often whine when they're emotionally frayed and lack the self-regulation to express themselves well. It's like a low battery alert from their nervous system.

✓ What Helps

You don't have to give in to whining or respond with frustration. You can hold the line while helping your child reset emotionally. Try saying:

- *"I want to understand you, but I need to hear your strong voice."*
- *"Let's take a breath together. You can try again with a calm voice."*

Responding in ways like these teaches your child that connection and communication go hand in hand. It also avoids reinforcing the idea that whining is the fastest way to get results.

✓ What to Avoid

- **Don't mock or mimic the tone.** It may feel tempting, but it often leads to shame.
- **Don't give in to end the noise.** This teaches that whining "works," so your child will try it again.

Stay steady. Acknowledge the need behind the behavior, hold your boundary, and guide them toward clearer communication.

Celebrate the Reset

When they try again with a calm voice, acknowledge them for it:

"That was such a clear way to ask. I really appreciate that."

"I love how you used your strong voice. That helped me understand you better."

If you praise like this, it reinforces the value of calm communication not just for today, but for life. You're not just reducing the whining. You're strengthening your child's ability to express their needs in healthy ways.

 Backtalk

"Whatever."
"You're not the boss of me."
"This is stupid."

Children talk back when they feel powerless or overwhelmed. It's a protest—clumsy, immature, but real. When kids feel overwhelmed, unheard, or cornered, their nervous system struggles to regain control. Sometimes that control looks like sarcasm, snark, or an outright challenge.

It might sound like, but it actually means:

- "You're so unfair." → I don't feel understood.
- "This is dumb." → I feel helpless.
- "You can't make me." → I need to feel in charge of something.
- "Whatever" → I feel anxious and vulnerable right now.

✓ What Helps

When backtalk occurs, your first instinct may be to shut down the behavior. Here's the key: resist the urge to power-match. Getting louder, stricter, or sarcastic may feel like taking control, but these reactions can escalate the tension instead of resolving it. Instead try:

"You can be upset, but we still speak respectfully."

"That sounded pretty harsh. Let's take a second and try again."

"It seems like something else is going on. Want to talk when we're both calm?"

This doesn't mean you're letting it slide. You're naming the boundary while also creating space for reflection.

✓ Look for Patterns

Backtalk often follows predictable stress points: after school, during transitions, when they feel criticized or micromanaged, and so on.

Noticing patterns helps you intervene earlier through connection instead of correction.

For example: *"Hey, I notice that you're pretty tense after school. Want a few minutes before we jump into homework to talk?"*

That small buffer can defuse tension before the snark arrives.

✓ Set Boundaries Without Shame

You can set a clear limit without turning it into a lecture:

- "I get that you're frustrated. I won't let us talk to each other this way."
- "We can disagree, but we'll do it respectfully."

Kids are still learning how to disagree without disrespect. Your calm, consistent modeling gives them a roadmap.

☑ Defiance

You ask them to get dressed. They don't move. You ask again. Still nothing. Now your voice sharpens: "Why aren't you listening?" And they stare, roll their eyes, or walk away.

It feels like defiance. Disrespect. A power struggle you didn't sign up for. But here's what most parents don't realize: **what looks like "won't" is often actually "can't."**

Sometimes kids seem defiant when they're overwhelmed by their feelings or surroundings. They might just need guidance to find their way through. Their brain goes into a freeze mode—not because they're plotting, but because they don't know how to respond.

Try naming what you see:

"It looks like you're having a hard time listening. Want to tell me what's up?"

"You're not ready to start yet—that's okay. I'll give you two minutes, and then we'll do it together."

It's important to avoid power struggles. Offer simple choices when possible. *"Do you want to brush your teeth now or after putting on the pajamas?"* Giving a sense of control often defuses resistance.

☑ Meltdowns

You said no to a second cookie, and now your child is on the floor, screaming. It escalated fast. Logic won't land, and nothing makes it stop. You feel like a hostage in your own kitchen. Meltdown gets too harsh; you validate their emotions and consequences, step back temporarily, and return.

Meltdowns are not manipulation. They're the result of a nervous system that's overstimulated. Your child's brain is overwhelmed, their body is overloaded, and they've lost access to regulation. Your child isn't giving you a hard time; they're having a hard time.

Don't try to reason during a meltdown. Instead, ground yourself and say:

- *"You're really upset. I'm right here."*
- *"Take your time. I'll stay with you until you're ready."*

This communicates that big emotions are allowed, and love isn't withdrawn when it gets messy. After the meltdown, revisit what happened: *"What do you think we can do differently next time?"* This builds emotional insight without shame.

From Chaos to Clarity

Everyday challenges—like sibling fights, whining, backtalk, or meltdowns—aren't signs that you're failing as a parent. They're signs that your child is still growing, practicing, and figuring it all out.

They don't need perfection from you, but they do need calm, connection, and clear guidance.

When you start seeing behavior as a form of communication, everything shifts. You stop taking it personally and parent from a position of strength rather than survival.

Remember, you don't need a perfect script. You just need to slow down, stay steady, and understand the person underneath the hard moment. Real discipline isn't about control, it's about connection. Every time you respond with empathy and structure, you're not just managing behavior, you're shaping character. You're building trust. You're teaching your child how to survive during their hardest days. And this is the kind of parenting that truly transforms.

When Repair Matters More Than Perfection

So far, we've covered many ways to stay calm, respond with empathy, and hold boundaries.

Let's be honest- sometimes you can't keep up with these strategies. You yell. You say something harsh. You slam the door. Later, the guilt creeps in: *Did I just undo everything I've worked so hard to build?*

1) Unpredictable Anger Hurts More

Kids can handle discipline. They can handle "no." What they struggle to handle is not knowing *which version of you* they will see. Calm? Explosive? Distant?

That unpredictability shakes their sense of safety.

Many child psychologists observe that the worst part for kids isn't the yelling, it's the unpredictability of it. When consequences feel random or reactions change with your mood, kids feel powerless. Such kids often protect themselves by disconnecting from others.

If you want to repair, a good place to start is by being more predictable. Not just when things are calm, but (especially) when they're hard.

2) "I'm Sorry" Isn't Enough

You might think, *If I apologize, they'll forget it.* But memory doesn't work that way, especially with kids.

What they remember the most isn't what happened, but how that made them feel. Intense emotional moments can deeply embed in their memory. If your outburst left them feeling scared, confused, or ashamed, a quick apology won't fully erase that.

If you **pair your apology with a small change**, it may not erase the memory for your child, but it might put what happened in perspective for them, and for you.

Try saying: "I didn't like how I yelled at you earlier. I'm working on my anger and will try to do better next time."

Next time, pause, breathe, and do one thing differently—even if it's just walking away before the blow-up.

Consistency rebuilds trust. Over time, your child learns that even when you mess up, they return to them. You care. You are trying.

That's repair. That's healing.

3) Fill The Relationship Bank

Your relationship is like a **savings account**. Every warm connection, shared laugh, and bedtime story is a deposit. Every harsh word or reactive moment is a withdrawal. Your goal isn't to avoid every withdrawal—it's to **have enough deposits** so that the hard moments don't bankrupt the relationship.

Here's how you can help that account grow:

- Take 5 minutes to play, fully present.
- Say, "I love being your parent," just because.
- Let your child hear you say, "I'm proud of who you're becoming."

When your relationship is strong, your child won't need perfection to feel safe. They'll know: *We have something real. Even when it's messy.*

Bottom line: Your child doesn't need a flawless parent. They need a steady one. One who owns their mistakes. One who comes back after a hard moment and says, "Let's try again." One who shows, over time, that love isn't erased by anger- it's rebuilt through repair.

Chapter 8 Recap:
Real Strategies for Real Challenges

1. What looks like **disrespect is often dysregulation**, not a character flaw.

2. **Everyday challenges** like lying, backtalk, or whining **are windows into unmet needs.**

3. **Responding to unwanted behavior with calm and clarity builds emotional safety.**

4. When you **model self-regulation,** you encourage your child to do so, too.

5. **Repair matters more than perfection.** A steady, respectful connection is what truly lasts.

CHAPTER 9

Magical Consequences

"Children must never work for our love; they must rest in it."
– Dr. Gordon Neufeld

Kids Understand More Than You Think

You might think your child is too young to understand it. Too little to grasp what you're saying. Too distracted to remember what happened yesterday. Here's what you need to know: **Kids understand more than you think, especially when it comes to boundaries, consequences, and how you show up for them.**

Children are incredibly attuned to the emotional environment around them. They may not always respond the way we want them to in the moment, but that doesn't mean they don't listen when you talk. It doesn't mean they're not learning. They're absorbing our tone, our follow-through, and our ability to stay calm—or not. They're learning what happens when they push limits and what it feels like when someone holds those limits with love instead of force.

You don't need to lecture or over-explain. In fact, the simpler your words and the more consistent your actions, the better your child will understand and internalize them.

With this in mind, let's reframe what discipline really is. It's not about overpowering your child or controlling them into better behavior. It's about **teaching**. It's about **modeling**. It's about showing them, *"This is how we do things in our family, even when it's hard."*

Children don't just learn through correction; they learn through connection, as well. Imagine if your partner greeted you with criticism the moment you walked in: "Why is this house a mess? What did you do all day?" This would create distance and defensiveness. Similarly, children pick up on cues of presence, calm, and clarity. When they consistently see you following through on your words, they build trust. This trust becomes their inner compass. Here's what your child really needs to know:

- That limits are there to keep them safe, not to punish them.
- That their big feelings are allowed, but hurtful behavior isn't.
- That no matter how upset they get, you'll stay in charge, lovingly, firmly, and with compassion.

When you lead that way, even the youngest child starts to feel it: **"My parent believes I can do better. And they're here to help me learn how."**

This is how respect is built. This is how emotional safety is created. And this is why discipline, if done well, isn't something we *do to* kids, it's something we do *with them*.

Consequences That Teach: THE 5 RS

Dr. Jane Nelsen, founder of Positive Discipline, developed the concept of the 5Rs: 5 guiding principles that help parents move from reactive punishment to meaningful guidance. Let's walk through them with real-world examples, simple scripts, and the science to back it up.

First, let's define discipline. It's not about making your child pay for a mistake; it's about helping them *learn* from it. How? By turning misbehavior into a teachable moment. Not through fear. Not through control. But through calm, clear guidance that helps your child feel seen, safe, and supported. When kids understand *why* a boundary matters, not just *what* it is, they're more likely to respect and remember it.

Let's take a closer look at how to incorporate teachable moments in real-life scenarios:

1. Related—Keep the Consequence Relatable

"No helmet, no bike."

The consequence should make sense in the context of the misbehavior. If your child doesn't wear a helmet when they ride their bike, your first instinct might be to take away dessert or screen time. However, disciplining them this way won't change the undesired behavior. Taking away bike-riding privileges is a more effective form of discipline as it helps them connect to the outcome.

Example:

"Hey, I noticed you didn't wear your helmet. That's not safe. No bike riding today, but tomorrow you can try again with the helmet on."

In this scenario, you're not punishing your child; your intention is to instill a behavior that protects them. It's about their *safety*. When the consequence matches the behavior, it feels fair and teaches responsibility.

Why it works: Research by the American Academy of Pediatrics shows that children learn most effectively through natural and logical consequences rather than arbitrary punishment.

2. Respectful–Lead Without Shaming

Guiding children with respect means setting boundaries without resorting to shame or guilt. We've all been there, frustrated and overwhelmed by our child's actions, and it's easy to let our emotions take over.

Consider these scenarios:

- **Common Reaction:** "Oh no, not again! You threw the puzzle pieces. I'm so tired of this. You're hopeless!"

This reaction may stem from exasperation, but it sends a message of shame and can leave the child feeling defeated.

- **Respectful Approach:** "I see you threw the puzzle pieces, so let's put them away for today. We can try again tomorrow."

Notice the shift? This response acknowledges your child's behavior without belittling them. It's about giving the child a space to learn and grow.

Sometimes staying calm is tough, and that's okay. You can own your emotions and take a breather:

"I'm a bit frustrated right now. Let's talk about what happened with the train tracks after dinner."

These examples show how a respectful tone fosters understanding and respect. As Dr. Laura Markham from *Aha! Parenting* notes, "When kids feel respected, they're more open to guidance." By choosing respect, you build an environment where your child feels safe to reflect on their actions and learn from them.

3. Reasonable–Match Your Reaction to the Moment

"I'll think through punishments before assigning them without thinking."

The goal isn't to make them suffer. It's to help them reflect. If your 4-year-old makes a mess, taking away their toys for a week is too harsh a punishment. It doesn't match the severity of the misbehavior. Rather, a short and focused break is appropriate.

Example:

For younger kids:

"You threw the puzzle. Take a break and try again tomorrow."

For older kids:

"Since you didn't finish your homework, let's skip video games tonight. How about we come up with a plan together to make sure it gets done next time?"

If the consequence is too long or intense, kids focus on the unfairness rather than the behavior. Consequences should feel like guiderails, not a punishment.

4. Revealed In Advance–Create Clarity, Not Confusion

"So, you know what to expect…"

Letting your child know what will happen next gives them a sense of control. They can choose the action and understand the result. When consequences are a surprise, they feel like punishment. When they know the outcomes ahead of time, they feel like they have structure.

Example:

"If the homework isn't finished by 7:30 p.m., there won't be time for games." Or:

"When I ask you to turn off the tablet, that's your 5-minute warning. If you keep playing after that, the tablet goes away for the next day."

This allows your child to participate in the boundary, giving them a sense of control. And it gives you peace of mind.

5. Repeated Back to You–Secure the Understanding

"Can you repeat the rule we agreed on?"

This step is powerful for younger children. When a child repeats the rule, they show you that they *understand* it. It moves the boundary from your head to theirs.

Example:

Parent: "So, what happens if you keep playing after I ask you to turn off the tablet?"

Child: "No tablet tomorrow."

Parent: "Right. Thanks for remembering."

⇨ For younger kids, keep it simple:

Parent: "What happens if we don't pick up the toys?"

Child: "They go in the basket."

This helps the child to take the ownership. If they break the rule, they know the consequence.

Parent Perspective: *"We used to fight every time I took away the iPad. But once my daughter started repeating the rule back to me, everything changed. She still tested me, but when I enforced the agreed-on consequence, she didn't feel betrayed. She knew the deal. And over time, she started to make better decisions."*

That's the difference between a punishment and a life lesson. That's the magic of consequences that teach.

Consistency Is Key

Boundaries are like lines on a road (literally and figuratively). They don't need to have iron spikes, but they need to stand out and remain visible at all times. When the lines move, kids don't know where to step safely. That's when misbehavior rises—not because they're "bad," but because they're unsure.

Even the best parenting tools—such as natural consequences or calming strategies—only work when they're applied consistently. Using a good strategy once or twice doesn't create change. Repetition is what rewires the brain.

Think about your own habits: You want to lose weight. You know what to eat, what not to eat, and what to do at the gym. But if you only follow that routine sometimes—eating well on Monday, then giving up by Thursday, the results don't come. Why? Because consistency leads to positive outcomes.

Children are no different. They thrive on structure. When you calmly follow through, even when it's hard, your child learns: "My parent means what they say. I can count on that."

That kind of consistency doesn't just reduce misbehavior, it builds safety. It says, "You're secure here. The rules are fair, and they're not going to disappear." No yelling. No lectures. Just calm, repeated leadership. That's how positive habits form. That's how trust grows.

Helping Your Child Express Big Feelings

We've talked about boundaries, consistency, and follow-through. Here's what ties it all together: A child who can name their feelings is a child who can eventually manage their behavior independently.

Most misbehavior starts with a big emotion that a child doesn't know how to express. Your child might yell, not because they're defiant but because they feel ignored. They might lie because they feel ashamed. They might shut down because they feel overwhelmed.

Emotional language is a skill that your child develops, and it needs to be taught to them.

You don't have to lecture. Just become your child's **emotional translator**, someone who helps them put words into what their body and brain are shouting about.

You might say:

"It sounds like you felt angry when Tim took your toy."

"Were you feeling left out when I hugged Christy and didn't hug you yet?"

These small translations help kids pause and process. They go from acting out to *figuring out* what's happening inside them.

Eventually, you can encourage them to try it themselves:

"I feel mad because you said no."

"I feel sad when no one listens to me."

Don't wait for a meltdown. If you teach emotional skills to your child when things are calm, they can draw on that knowledge when things are messy. Practice during story time. Model during your own tough moments:

"I'm getting frustrated, so I'm going to take a breath."

The more you teach emotional language, the more you give your child something powerful—not just a way to behave better, but a way to understand themselves. And that is truly magical.

Chapter 9 Recap:

Magical Consequences

1. **Your child understands more than you think.** They learn not just from what you say, but from what you do.

2. Consequences are most powerful when they are directly related to the misbehavior.

3. The **5Rs of respectful consequences (Related, Reasonable, Revealed in advance, Respectful, Repeated)** build trust and accountability.

4. When it comes to discipline, **consistency creates clarity and safety.** Clear, predictable boundaries help children feel secure.

5. Helping kids name and express their feelings builds **emotional awareness and control**.

6. When you **act as an emotional translator,** you don't just manage behavior, you teach your child lifelong skills for self-understanding and connection.

Building Connection

Part IV

CHAPTER 10

CONNECTION B4 CORRECTION

"When in doubt, choose connection." – Dr. Becky Kennedy

Let's take a breath here.

If you've made it this far, it shows that you're a dedicated parent who is committed to building a deeper, stronger connection with your child. And you absolutely can.

This chapter is devoted to **connection**, a principle so powerful that it's the title of one of my previous books, *Connection Before Correction*. Here, you'll discover how prioritizing connection can change everything. We'll delve into exactly how connection works and how to form a lasting, genuine bond with your child.

How Connection Works

What does connection mean to you?

For some parents, connecting with their child might seem like it's all about being liked or sharing fun moments. While these aspects are enjoyable, true connection goes much deeper. A key component of connection is a shared sense of emotional safety: *"I am seen, I matter, I belong, even when I mess up."*

Connection isn't about avoiding correction. It's what makes correction *work*.

Connect, Then Redirect

Imagine you're upset after a hard day. Your partner walks in and after a brief exchange, says, *"Well, you should've just said no to the extra meeting,"* or *"You're overreacting."* How would you feel? Probably defensive, or hurt. It's likely that you might not be in a mental space to receive advice (no matter how well-meaning that advice might be).

Now, imagine your spouse sits next to you after you explain why you're upset, and they say, *"That sounds like a really hard day. I get why you're feeling this way."* You breathe. Your guard drops. You feel safe. When you feel seen, you have the space to think clearly again.

This also applies to your child. Their brains can't absorb correction until they feel emotionally safe. Their nervous system has to shift out of fight-or-flight before they can hear what you're saying. This is why yelling doesn't work in the long term. Even well-reasoned, logical thinking doesn't stand a chance unless a connection is established first.

Dr. Dan Siegel, a clinical professor of psychiatry at the UCLA School of Medicine and the executive director of the Mindsight Institute, refers to this concept as *"connect and redirect."* It's a simple idea, but it's one of the most powerful tools we have as parents: Connect emotionally first, then redirect the behavior.

How's Your Connection with Your Child?

Think of your relationship with your child like a Wi-Fi signal: When it's strong, communication flows effortlessly, and everyone feels in sync. However, if it's weak, communication gets lost, leading to frustration on both sides. The key to rebuilding that signal is empathy and understanding. When you truly empathize with your child, their feelings are acknowledged and validated, creating a space for genuine connection.

Here's how it works in real life: Imagine your child shouts, "You're the worst!" because you had to cancel a planned sleepover that your child had with a friend. Instead of reacting with anger, over explanation, or punishment, pause, get down to their level, and softly respond with something like this: "I can see you're really disappointed. You've been looking forward to that sleepover all day, and it hurts to hear 'no'. I get it."

That's true connection: You've empathized with your kid by showing that you understood their emotions, made them feel seen, and opened the door for calmer dialogue. Once the moment passes and everyone's calm, you can guide them forward by saying, "Let's figure out a better way to express those big feelings next time."

This approach doesn't ignore boundaries. It shows that empathy and accountability can coexist, strengthening your bond while teaching valuable lessons.

What About a Strong-Willed Child?

"Okay, but what if my kid is different?"

"What if nothing I do works?"

"What if connection just isn't enough?"

If this is your case, rest assured that you're not doing anything wrong. This section is for parents who have tried the tools laid out so far in this book but still feel stuck. For parents who are wondering, 'What now?'

Strong Wills, Strong Feelings

Strong-willed kids are often bright, sensitive, and feel their emotions deeply. They typically don't like being told what to do and won't comply *just because you say so*. They crave **autonomy**, **respect**, and **authenticity**.

They'll push back hard if they feel controlled, even if your intentions are loving. They often require explanations, negotiations, and clarifications.

Here's the hard truth, and it's nothing to be ashamed of or embarrassed about: Strong-willed kids often bring out the worst in us. Not because we're bad parents. But because their intensity pulls out our own childhood wounds, control patterns, and unmet needs.

Partnering In Parenting

Connection still matters. It always matters. But for strong-willed kids, efforts towards consistency need to be:

- **More persistent:** Maintain consistent boundaries even amidst challenges.
- **More genuine:** Approach interactions with authenticity to build trust.
- **Less about control:** Prioritize collaboration over authority.

Try this:

"I see that you really want to do it your way. I'm here to help you through it, not force it on you."

This small shift, from power *over* to power *with*, can completely change the vibe of the moment. It disarms the battle before it starts. Strong-willed kids crave partnership and respect rather than management.

That's why threats and punishments often backfire. Strong-willed kids will double down because they want to feel a sense of power and control. Instead of escalating the situation, offer choices to them. Use collaborative language like, "Let's figure this out together." Keep your tone calm but firm. You're not giving up your authority; you're showing them what effective leadership looks like.

When Connections Don't Work, Seek Support

There are notable differences between a strong-willed child and a child whose behavior is deeply disruptive, aggressive, or impacting daily life.

If you feel:

- Nothing you do seems to help.
- Your child's meltdowns are extreme or unsafe.
- You often feel scared, hopeless, or stuck.

Don't try to "fix it" alone. That's not failure. That's wisdom.

Working with a child therapist, behavior specialist, or pediatric psychologist can provide insight and strategies tailored to your child's unique needs. You wouldn't wait to treat a broken bone. Similarly, don't wait to support your child's mental health (or yours). Sometimes the most loving thing we can do for them, and for ourselves, is to ask for help.

Strong-willed kids aren't broken. They're wired for intensity. That intensity requires support, structure, and connection—sometimes with some professional help.

When you ask for help, it doesn't mean that you've failed. In fact, it is quite the opposite. It means that you're building a village, and your child deserves all your love and support. You're doing a brave thing. It's not easy to keep showing up for a child who challenges you. But you still do. That's love. That's strength. That's what will foster a stronger connection between you and your child.

Discovering What Fills Your Child's Tank

Have you ever heard of a "love tank?" Everyone, child or adult, has a love tank. It's a way to describe the extent to which we feel loved and fulfilled. Understanding your child's "love tank" is essential for addressing their emotional needs and helping them thrive. They may display resilience, adaptability, and connection. When your child's emotional tank is full, they are able to manage disappointments and recover from setbacks in a better way.

When their tank runs low, even a simple request from you may trigger a meltdown in them. This type of behavior often stems from your child's emotional needs, not intentional defiance. Meeting their emotional needs through play, quality time, words of affirmation, physical affection, and acts of service ensures their emotional tank is replenished.

Identify what makes your child light up or calms them down. Offering small gestures—such as an extra hug, playful interaction, or attentive listening—builds trust and connection, fostering a lifelong bond.

Ways to Fill Your Child's Love Tank

- **Play**: Engage in activities that spark joy and connection. Organize a living room dance party, have a pillow fight, or create a silly puppet show. These moments of play not only entertain but also strengthen your bond.

- **Quality Time**: It's not about endless hours, but meaningful minutes. Turn cooking dinner into a fun project that you can do together or have a bedtime chat about their day. Focused moments where you're all in—without distractions—make them feel truly loved.

- **Words of Affirmation**: Boost their confidence with specific praise. Instead of just saying "Good job," try "I loved how you shared with your sibling today." Your words shape their self-view and inspire confidence in them.

- **Physical Affection**: Simple touches convey deep support. Start their day with a hug or a kiss. Hold their hand during a walk. These small gestures reassure them that they're secure and cherished.

- **Acts of Service**: Show care through helpful acts. Surprise them with their favorite breakfast or help pack their school bag for the next day. These actions speak volumes about your love and consideration.

Grab a pen and paper and answer these questions:

- When does your child light up?
- When do they lean in?
- When do they calm down and soften?

When your child is acting out, refer to this list to see how you can meet them where they are by filling their emotional tank.

You can't always ensure that your child's emotional tanks are completely full every day. That's just not possible. Some days are busy. Some days are hard. However, if you know what fills your child's tank, even just one or two things, you can start offering it. One extra hug. One silly voice. One minute of eye contact at bedtime.

Those acts may seem small, but they add up over time. The kids who *feel* loved are the kids who *listen* better, cooperate more, and trust your guidance.

By consistently filling their tank, you're not just easing the moment; you're building a bond that lasts a lifetime.

Repair After Yelling

Now let's talk about repair. How do you normally mend things after you lose your calm and have an outburst? Do you brush it off as if nothing happened, or do you offer them a genuine apology?

When life's daily stresses spill over into a yelling outburst, the anger behind it often fades and is quickly followed by shame or guilt. Thoughts like, "I ruined everything," or "They'll never forget this moment," can haunt us. But as we've covered throughout this book, yelling doesn't have to be the end of the story. What truly matters is what comes next—the repair.

Why Repair Matters So Much

When you lose your temper (and every parent does), your child might feel scared, confused, or even responsible for your reaction. If we don't say anything, they're left to make sense of it alone. That silence can lead to self-blame—both yours and theirs.

- *"Maybe it was my fault."*
- *"Mom's mad because I'm too much."*
- *"I can't make Dad happy."*

When you make the effort to revisit and repair what happened, you rewrite the story. You are demonstrating to them that even when things get messy, we can come back together. We can heal.

You show them:

- Emotions don't ruin relationships.
- Apologies matter, and grown-ups can admit their mistakes.
- Love isn't fragile; it can deal with hard moments.

Don't think, "Do I really need to apologize to my child?" Remember, even young children understand and feel more than we realize. Apologizing doesn't weaken your authority; it strengthens trust. It shows that love isn't conditional on perfection and proves how strong your bond is.

What A Real Repair Sounds Like

You don't need a perfect speech. Just honesty, softness, and presence.

You might say:

- "I got overwhelmed and yelled. That wasn't okay. I'm really sorry."
- "You didn't deserve to be spoken to like that."
- "It wasn't your fault. I'm working on staying calm when I feel big feelings."

And then: Stop talking. Let it land. No lectures. No over-explaining. Just presence. Perhaps offer a hug, a few quiet moments beside each other, or gently ask:

"How did that feel for you when I yelled?" (Only ask this if you're regulated and ready to listen without defending.)

What Does Repair Teach Your Child?

When you repair, you model emotional responsibility and instill self-awareness in your child. You teach them that:

- Mistakes are part of relationships.
- You don't have to be perfect to be loved.
- It's safe to tell the truth about hard things.

You show them that love isn't erased by hard moments. You show them that love becomes stronger through honesty and reconnection. If you believe that yelling makes you a bad parent, then you need to let that go. Refusing to repair afterward? That's where disconnection lingers.

So next time you yell, remember: It's never too late to go back and say, *"I'm sorry. You matter. I'm still here."* This is what stays with them.

Daily Rituals That Maintain Connection

You don't need grand gestures to build strong bonds with your child. Sometimes it's the quiet, consistent acts that speak the loudest. That little hand squeeze before school. The same silly joke every bedtime. A quick *"What made you smile today?"* over dinner. These aren't just habits, they're *rituals*. Rituals create rhythm, safety, and a sense of belonging.

They assure your child: *"No matter how messy today was, we still have us."*

What Rituals Might Look Like

Tiny acts, done consistently, build safety and connection. They don't have to be fancy, just predictable.

Here are some simple ideas:

- Give your child a morning hug before the morning routine starts (e.g., getting dressed, brushing teeth, etc.).
- Start and maintain a 3-minute cuddle at bedtime. If your child is older, consider having a nightly chat about their day or sharing a favorite chapter from a book together.
- A movie session every Friday night (or whatever works for your schedule).
- Drawing or painting together for 10 minutes a week.

- If they're younger, sing their favorite song to them every night (even if you think you sing badly, they won't mind!)

✏️ Now it's your turn! List 3 new rituals that you might want to try with your child.

These moments work not because you execute them perfectly, but because they're *predictable*. Predictability builds trust. Even when everything feels chaotic, your rituals are the steady heartbeat underneath.

Think of these rituals as a way to employ the concept of quality over quantity: It's not how much time you give, but what you do with that time.

Chapter 10 Recap:

Connection Before Correction

1. **When your child feels emotionally safe, the stage is set for you to have a greater connection** with them.

2. There are many ways to **fill your child's emotional tank** and foster a connection with them. Some of these include: Playtime, quality time, acts of service, physical affection, and words of affirmation.

3. **It's never too late to repair after yelling.** By modeling the importance of a sincere apology after you make a mistake, you subtly show your child that no one is perfect and asking for an apology isn't a sign of weakness.

4. **Enact rituals that help to maintain your connection** with your child, like cuddling at bedtime, movie nights, and more.

CHAPTER 11

WHEN YOU AND YOUR PARTNER CLASH

"It's not about being the same—it's about being on the same team."
– Unknown

Your Own Worst Critic

Perhaps before having kids, you and your partner rarely clashed. One of you liked routines, the other didn't mind messes. It worked. But once parenting entered the picture, every small difference started to feel like a big one. Things like tone of voice, bedtime routines, or how to respond to backtalk turned into full-blown arguments. You're both trying to do your best, but it feels like you're both speaking different languages.

You might wonder, how *can two people who love each other so much feel so far apart on parenting?*

It isn't that something is wrong with you or them. You were shaped by different stories, cultures, families, and learning experiences that defined what "love" and "safety" meant to you. And that's okay.

Why Parenting Differences Feel So Personal

Parenting doesn't just bring out your instincts—it activates your oldest emotional wiring. One of you may naturally lean toward connection: *"They're having a hard time."* The other may lean toward control and discipline: *"They need to learn a lesson."* Neither is wrong. You're both trying to protect something that matters.

When your partner does things differently, it can feel more than just annoying, it can feel very personal. Why? Because parenting taps into your internal blueprint. How you were raised shapes how you give love, seek safety, and respond to stress.

Perhaps you were raised in a home where obedience meant safety, and where talking back was not only rude but also dangerous. So, when your child snaps back, it lights a fire in your chest. Meanwhile, your partner shrugs it off and says, "It's not a big deal." That difference? It can feel personal, even if it's not.

Even if you and your partner come from the same town, speak the same language, or share the same faith, you were each raised in a different emotional culture. One household might have taught: "Speak only when spoken to." The other household said, "Say what you feel."

When you argue about tone, routines, or consequences, it's not really about parenting. It's about identity. It's about safety. It's about what love looked like when you were small. That's why small disagreements can feel so big. It's not just about the shoes on the floor or the bedtime routine, it's about whose method feels right, and whose method feels wrong.

But there's good news: Different doesn't mean incompatible. You both bring value. You both have blind spots. The goal isn't to parent in the same way; it's to understand each other's viewpoints so you can work as a team.

✏️ When you and your partner have some 1:1 time together, take the time to write out the answers to the following questions. The answers will help you gain a deeper understanding of where you're coming from.

- *"What are we both trying to protect?"*
- *"What kind of emotional environment do we want in our home?"*
- *"How can we use both of our strengths to lead together?*

These questions aren't about finding the "right" answer. They're about building a bridge that lets you both stand side by side, even when your instincts don't match. A bridge where your child feels safe, supported, and truly loved.

Recognizing Parenting Roles

As we explored in the previous section, in parenting, one partner may naturally lean more softly while the other leans more firmly. One worries about preserving connection, while the other is more concerned about building character.

Let's look at how these differences show up and how to work with them, rather than against them.

- **Partner 1**: *"Jamie said she doesn't want to go to violin again. Why are you pushing her?"*

- **Partner 2**: *Because she said the same thing about swimming lessons, and now she loves it. Sometimes we have to push her to do hard things."*

The argument begins in the car on the way to violin practice, again. She feels like he's undermining her structure. He feels like she's ignoring their daughter's voice. And by the time they arrive, no one is calm.

If this feels familiar, you're not alone. One parent leans toward pushing for growth, and the other leans toward honoring feelings. One is trying to raise a resilient child; the other is trying to raise an emotionally secure one. No one is right or wrong in these scenarios, and realizing it is the first step towards parenting as partners.

The Critic and The Softie in Action

In many couples, one parent is **"The Critic"**—firm, clear, and structured. The other is **"The Softie"**—compassionate, flexible, and nurturing. These roles aren't right or wrong; they're simply different approaches, often shaped by their own upbringing.

Think about it: are you the one who values structure and feels uneasy with chaos? Or are you the nurturing type, worried that too much pressure might harm trust and connection? These dynamics often reflect our deeper values and fears.

This is how disagreements over parenting approaches often arise. Perhaps one parent insists on "no dessert until the homework is done." The other might sneak a cookie to prevent a tantrum. One parent strictly enforces screen time rules, only for the other to say, "Just five more minutes." One insists on follow-through; the other suggests, "Pick your battles." These moments aren't about one parent being "right" and the other being "wrong," but rather about two different perspectives unfolding.

Research consistently tells us: Kids need both structure and softness. Dr. Diana Baumrind, renowned for her work on authoritative parenting at the University of California, found that the healthiest outcomes emerge from parents who skillfully combine high expectations with high warmth. This isn't about you and your partner parenting in the exact same way. Instead, it's about recognizing and respecting what each of you is trying to protect and achieve through your own unique approach. This understanding is the critical step in moving from competition to collaboration.

Recognizing the roles isn't about labeling each other; it's about exploring how both perspectives can genuinely enrich your parenting and foster resilient, emotionally secure children. To start bridging these differences and building a stronger parenting team, try asking each other these powerful questions. Consider adding your own unique relationship and experiences to the discussion:

To understand where the other person is coming from, try asking each other the following questions. Add your own questions that are unique to your relationship and experiences:

- *"What are you afraid will happen if we don't hold this line?"*
- *"What are you hoping our child will feel in this moment?"*

When you start asking, not assuming, you soften the story you've written about each other. You stop seeing your partner as the problem, and you start seeing ways to build a parenting team where both your voices matter.

Your Partner Isn't Your Opponent

You chose your partner for all the dreams and shared values you saw in them. But amid school runs and long routines, you may feel more like opponents. Exhaustion sets in, and every disagreement feels like a battle: "Why am I always the bad guy?" "Why do you keep undermining me in front of the kids?"

You may both be asking yourselves, silently or out loud, *how did we get here?*

When Parenting Reveals the Cracks

Parenting often highlights areas in a relationship that need attention. It can bring out hidden expectations and past experiences, reflecting the different backgrounds and lessons each of you learned while growing up. Perhaps one of you experienced strict discipline, while the other had more permissive parents. These differing histories shape your parenting instincts.

When these approaches intersect, deep-seated beliefs and past experiences can create a strained environment. This can lead to clashes where your child is unintentionally caught in the middle.

Your child might be confused, asking themselves: *"Who do I listen to?" "Who's right?" "Did I cause this?"* Some kids act out. Some shut down. Some become people-pleasers, trying to keep the peace.

Fostering A "Same Jersey" Mentality

You and your partner aren't on opposite teams. You're wearing the same jersey. You're raising the same child. This doesn't mean you always agree. It means you choose to back each other up in the moment and have harder conversations later, when emotions are less volatile.

When discussing disagreements, aim for understanding rather than confrontation:

Instead of: "*Why do you always…*"
☺ Try: "*Can you share what you were thinking?*"

Instead of: "You're too soft,"
☺ Try: "*Can we talk about what felt important to you there?*"

Often, the parent who spends the most time with the kids might feel that they have all the answers. It's easy to fall into the trap of thinking, "I know the best." But dismissing your partner's input can lead to burnout and loneliness on both sides. Parenting is a marathon, not a sprint.

Your partner's perspective brings valuable insights. Keep the conversation flowing by discussing your core values and parenting goals. Embrace teamwork. After all, even star athletes rely on a team to succeed. The collective wisdom and love that you both contribute enriches your child's world.

Celebrate your partner's contributions. Together, you're creating something beautiful—a team that's raising a child out of shared love and dedication.

Your child doesn't need perfect parents. They need parents who can disagree with respect, stay steady in hard moments, and return to each other every time.

Same-Page Parenting

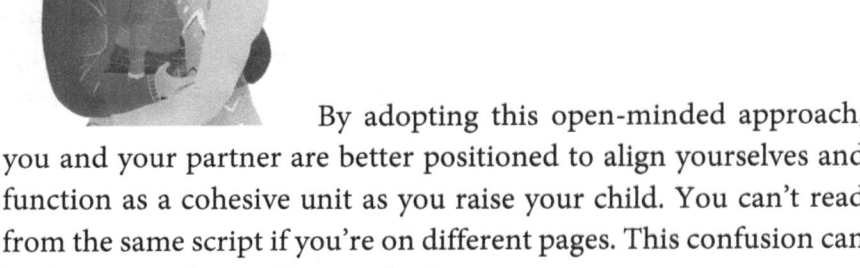

By adopting this open-minded approach, you and your partner are better positioned to align yourselves and function as a cohesive unit as you raise your child. You can't read from the same script if you're on different pages. This confusion can lead to misunderstandings and mistrust.

Rather than responding to your child's behavior in two conflicting directions, it's crucial for you and your partner to be on the same page. While it's okay to handle small everyday matters individually, it's imperative to uphold a united front on core issues.

In the spirit of working together, consider these agreements: If one parent sets a boundary, the other backs it up in front of the child. Discuss any disagreements privately later and avoid arguing about discipline in front of your kid. Use each other's names to show unity, like saying: "Mom and I decided this together."

These simple shifts protect more than the rules; they safeguard your child's emotional stability. Children thrive when they know what to expect, not just from one parent but from both. When you parent with unity, even when you disagree in private, your child feels anchored. They trust the structure, test boundaries less, and relax into the emotional safety of knowing: "My parents are working together."

When Parents Don't Match, Kids Get Mixed Signals

Imagine this: You have two supervisors. They each give you feedback on a project you are working on, but the feedback is contradictory. You'd feel confused, right? Whose instructions should you follow? You might even end up choosing the easier path for yourself, simply because the mixed messages are overwhelming. This example mirrors what children experience when parents aren't on the same page.

Children don't need perfect parents, but they do need consistent ones. When one parent sets a limit and the other overrides it, your child won't think, "I respect both of my parents." Instead, they'll wonder, "Whose side should I choose?" This uncertainty leads to your child pushing boundaries and misbehaving—not because they are "bad," but because they are unsure where the boundaries lie.

When boundaries shift based on parental presence, children don't feel more freedom, but they do feel less secure. It might appear as though they're taking advantage of the softer parent, but beneath that behavior lies uncertainty. Kids aren't equipped to thrive in unpredictability. They require clear, consistent boundaries they can trust, regardless of which parent is present.

When the rules change consistently, it's like walking on a bridge that keeps wobbling. It's not empowering, it's unsettling. Often, your child's misbehavior is just a way of asking: *"Can I trust you to hold the line?"*

What's Your Non-Negotiable?

The next time the house is finally quiet, and the day has settled, sit down with your partner and write down the answers to these questions:

- What matters the most to us when it comes to raising our child?
- What are the values we want to lead with?
- Where do we need to sync up so that we don't quietly resent each other every time a boundary is tested?

You don't need 50 rules. You just need a few shared anchors and a shared commitment to stand beside each other when it matters the most. Because you're not just raising a child; you're building the emotional foundation they'll stand on for life.

Chapter 11 Recap:
When You and Your Partner Clash

1. **You and your partner may have different approaches to parenting—that's ok!** Having open discussions about these differences is the first step to achieving same-page parenting.

2. Are you **the Critic or the Softie?**

3. When you **start asking and stop assuming**, your communication with your partner and parenting decisions improve.

4. When you and your partner send **mixed signals**, your child may become confused and/or misbehave.

5. **Strong parenting teams respect each other, set shared boundaries, and handle disagreements privately.**

CHAPTER 12

BE THE PARENT YOU WANT TO BE

"At the end of the day, the most overwhelming key to a child's success is the positive involvement of parents."
– Jane D. Hull

What Your Child Will Remember the Most

Have you ever imagined the day you drop your child off at their college dorm? The drive home is enveloped in unexpected silence. The morning's whirlwind of packing and farewells left little time for reflection; now the quiet brings questions:

- *Did I spend enough time with them?*
- *Why didn't we go on more family trips?*

- *Why did I let the little things bother me so much?*

Regret has a loud voice in quiet moments like this. In hindsight, you might see ordinary moments you once considered inconvenient as gifts.

Your child's future self won't remember every small detail, like what they wore on the first day of third grade, or the meals you prepared. Instead, they'll remember the love and warmth that surrounded them.

They'll cherish the comfort of your arms after a bad dream and your encouraging smile from the sidelines. They'll hold dear the nights you sat by their bed and said, "I love you, no matter what." Home will be remembered as a place of safety and authenticity, where love prevailed despite life's challenges.

Parenting is composed of small parts that come together to form a bigger whole. It's in the tiny, quiet moments—the look in your eyes when they needed comfort, and the tone of your voice when they were scared.

They'll remember the special soup you made when they were sick. The funny cake you baked that collapsed in the middle but still made them laugh. The quiet Sunday afternoon fishing with Dad, when the sunlight made the water shimmer like glass. It's those small, ordinary but sacred moments that stick.

The Power of Showing Up

Have you ever scanned the audience at a school performance, longing to see your parents' faces? I vividly recall my 2nd-grade play about the four food groups, standing on stage dressed as a shiny red apple. While my grandparents beamed at me from the second row, I kept searching for my parents. They finally arrived, flustered and late. I didn't need speeches or flowers; I just needed them to be present, on time, looking at me.

This moment left a lasting impression. It wasn't that my parents didn't care, they were simply stretched thin. But it taught me something profound: Being present matters.

As a parent, it's easy to feel the pressure to do everything perfectly. Yet, perfection isn't the goal; presence, physically and emotionally, is important. Your child senses when you're distracted or checked out. What they truly crave is for us to be genuinely attentive to them.

We can do this by tuning in to their world. Look at your child when they speak, not at your phone. Stay with them through their emotional storms and let them know that you'll always be there when things get tough. Your authenticity is more valuable than you trying to be the perfect parent.

When we show up, we're conveying more than what our words ever can. We're saying: "I see you. I hear you. You are important."

Dr. Dan Siegel and Dr. Tina Payne Bryson emphasize that "showing up" is a cornerstone of parenting. It fosters secure attachment, trust, and resilience. When we're consistently present for our children, they learn that they're worthy of attention, they can trust others to remain by their side, and that their emotions are valid.

Even if we can't get it right every time, it's about returning and staying emotionally engaged, especially during challenging times. These moments teach them: "When I needed my parents, they were present." This powerful, ongoing demonstration of care builds lasting connections.

Letting Go of Guilt

Imagine meeting a fellow parent named Tom. His eyes carry the weight of guilt as he speaks softly about his son Ryan, who has started to challenge the boundaries of adolescence. The echoes of a painful divorce and long working hours amplify Tom's guilt. Tom describes how, feeling inadequate, he backed away, relinquishing his role out of fear that he no longer had the right to lead and be a parent.

Guilt—a familiar companion for many parents—creeps in, whispering doubts about our choices and portrayals of ideal parenthood. It disguises itself as care, urging us to overcompensate and chase perfection. But reality tells a different story: parenting from a place of guilt distances us from our child.

Unchecked guilt can overshadow the joy of parenting, forcing us to turn inward when our children, in their raw authenticity, need us to be fully present. When you parent from guilt, decisions stem from a place of fear and self-doubt rather than from love and understanding.

Reclaiming Your Role

Let's be clear: Guilt isn't all bad. It can be a cue, a nudge that something needs attention. It's a **signal**, not a steering wheel.

Here's how to shift from guilt to grounded parenting:

1. **Name the guilt.** Naming it out loud takes away its power.

    "I feel guilty for missing the moments that mattered."

2. **Forgive yourself.** Accept your humanity with compassion. Your child needs your authentic presence, not a facade of perfection.

    "I was doing the best I could with what I knew."

3. **Be Present in the moment.** Shift your focus to the present. Look forward to connecting today, rather than dwelling on yesterday's missteps.

    "What does my child need from me at this very moment?"

4. **Parent from your values, not your emotions.** Ask yourself, especially after a hard day, where your decision comes from, and if it's really helping you be the parent that you want to be.

    "Am I doing this from a place of guilt, or thoughtful parenting?"

Keep returning with an open heart, a steady voice, and your values at the forefront. Even when it's messy, even when you wonder if it's working, it matters more than you know.

That's not performance. That's parenting. That's love in real time.

Parenting With Intention

Are You the Kind of Parent You Thought You'd Be?

It's a tough but important question. When we become new parents, we aspire to be great ones. As time passes, our self-imposed expectations become unrealistic, and we're left wondering what kind of parent we actually are, compared to the perfect parent we had in mind. This lack of concrete identity can lead to moments where, amidst the pressures of parenting, we react instinctively and later seek solutions for behaviors we didn't anticipate.

The importance of clearly establishing a parenting identity cannot be overstated. This identity shapes your parenting style and provides you with a direction. We tend to act in alignment with our thoughts, and without a clear sense of how we intend to parent, we often revert to familiar habits. Herein lies the power of intention. Intentional steps lead to actionable changes.

Teaching your children to respect healthy boundaries and encouraging them positively requires forethought. Similarly, handling your emotions in difficult situations demands a premeditated strategy. Without this, we succumb to innate responses, habitual actions, and perpetuating cycles we may wish to break.

You can still become the parent you had in mind, but in a more realistic way. Not by doing more, but by becoming more intentional about *who you want to be* and *how you want to show up*.

We talked about this in earlier chapters, but it's worth mentioning again here: Being a present parent isn't about the **amount of time** you spend with your kids. It's about the **quality** of the moments you share. Your child doesn't need 10 uninterrupted hours of your attention every day. Just a few minutes of genuine connection goes a long way.

✎ To get in touch with your ideal version of a parent, grab that pen and paper and ask yourself the following:

- *"What would I want to see myself doing?"*
- *"What do I want my kids to feel when they're with me?"*
- *"What values do I want to intentionally uphold, through words and actions, for my child?"*

Let those answers guide you. The parent your child needs the most is already inside you. Now, you have the tools to let that parent take the lead—not your guilt, not comparison, and not someone else's parenting style

Start Where You Are

Becoming the parent you want to be doesn't require a complete life overhaul. You can start today—right in this moment. Get fully engaged in the present moment, develop a keen awareness of your interactions, and make deliberate choices that align with your core values.

Here are small but powerful ways to begin:

- **Invest in yourself**–Remember that emotional regulation concept we covered in Chapter 4? That's an important one. Rest, journal, take a walk, read a book. You matter too. Emotionally regulated parents create emotionally regulated children.

- **Commit to less**–Say no to what drains you, so you can say yes to what truly matters.

- **Take breaks**–Allowing yourself to pause isn't quitting, it's replenishing your energy. Step away, breathe, and refuel when needed.

- **Start something new**–As we covered in Chapter 10, small rituals can hold great meaning. Consider a 5-minute story time or Sunday bike rides. Rituals need not be grand to be significant.

- **Reach out**–Seeking therapy or parent coaching isn't a sign of weakness, it's a sign of wisdom.

Parenting isn't solely about raising your child; it's a journey where you grow alongside them. It's about **becoming** the version of you that your child can trust, rely on, and learn from. You won't always get it right. But every time you pause and ask yourself, *"Who do I want to be right now for my child?"* you're one step closer to becoming that person.

Progress, Not Perfection

Think about someone learning to play a musical instrument. They start by understanding the fundamentals, identifying challenges, and recognizing which techniques help them improve. Their aim isn't to instantly master every piece but to make consistent progress, one note at a time. They embrace mistakes as learning opportunities and make deliberate choices to keep practicing and refining their skills.

Parenting is almost the same. You've learned that connection fosters growth more than control. But knowing isn't doing, especially when life's stresses challenge your resolve. When things go awry, remember, it's not failure. You're in the midst of growth where real change takes root. You're working to unlearn inherited patterns, and that effort is an incredible achievement.

Small Wins in Everyday Moments

Science shows us that relationships are built through the repetition of small, everyday interactions. While significant events can create memorable moments, it's really the regular, heartfelt exchanges that shape secure bonds over time. Your child needs a series of these emotionally attuned moments spread throughout their growing years.

It's normal to feel a bit awkward as you try new ways of connecting with your child. Progress often involves some setbacks—taking a step back after two steps forward. But every time you choose to be present, mend disconnections, and truly listen, you're creating something meaningful. These small actions are more impactful than you might think.

It's the small wins gathered over time that build the strongest connections. As you focus on these moments, you're not just parenting, you're crafting a lifelong bond and providing your child with a foundation of love and security. Keep cherishing these everyday victories, knowing they are the true essence of a loving and resilient family.

Chapter 12 Recap:
Be the Parent You Want to Be

1. Your child won't remember everything, but they will remember how they felt with you. What stays with them is **safety, warmth, and presence.**
2. You don't need perfect words or timing. Showing up with **honesty and emotional availability is what builds long-term trust.**
3. **Guilt and comparison disconnect us from our children.** Instead of performing for approval, lead from your values and reconnect with your "why."
4. **Parenting with intention means noticing your reactions and choosing to be the parent that you want to be**.
5. Progress is powerful. When you model reflection, repair, and consistency, you're not only transforming your relationship with your child—you're shaping their emotional future.

"Don't worry that children never listen to you; worry that they are always watching you."

— *Robert Fulghum*

CONCLUSION

You're the One They'll Come Back To

If you were to read only one sentence from this book, this might be the most valuable: *<u>If you foster an ongoing conversation of love, learning, and perseverance with your child, that's how you can stop yelling, and start connecting.</u> *

Parenting is a journey filled with twists, turns, and discoveries. As your child grows, your methods and understanding of what works best also changes. Remember, there's no need to strive for perfection. By embracing the ideas in this book, you offer your child a safe harbor—a place where they can find comfort when life gets stormy.

We've delved into concepts surrounding yelling, emotional regulation, and importance of boundaries. Perhaps you saw yourself in the "parent perspectives" or felt a personal connection to certain topics. You're transforming these insights into a new approach—**Connections Over Control**. Whether you grew up in a strict household or not, you're now choosing empathy and curiosity over criticism.

By pausing and apologizing when needed, you demonstrate strength through vulnerability—exactly what your child need.

To be a safe harbor for your child, you must manage your own emotions while parenting. We can't expect our children to control their emotions if we can't control ours. We all want our children to grow up happy and healthy. Happy parents create happy children, and parents who can regulate their emotions raise children who can do the same.

Parenting is tough. On some mornings, everything seems perfect; other times, it falls apart before breakfast is over. Regardless of the day, every effort you make to improve your parenting, large and small, strengthens the bond that you have with your child.

Fostering Independence Through Love

The ultimate goal of parenting is to prepare your child for their independence. How do you envision your child navigating the world beyond your embrace? You wish for them to build meaningful relationships and pursue their passions confidently. To achieve this, you must provide them with a robust, emotional framework—a legacy of mental health and resilience.

You're not just raising a child; you're cultivating a lifelong relationship with them and serving as a model for how they will engage in relationships with others.

Your child will cherish the safety of your presence more than the sharpness of your discipline, the warmth of your gaze over the weight of expectations. Being an aware, engaged parent isn't about the perfect moments (although it's certainly nice when that happens), but about fostering a space where unconditional love prevails.

When doubt creeps in and you're questioning whether you're doing enough, remember: You are. You're here. You care. You're trying. And that matters more than anything.

Challenges will come—meltdowns, eye rolls, backtalk. But now that you're equipped with awareness, language, and a clear vision of the parent you aspire to be, you are evolving with every thoughtful repair.

You are the safe base, the emotional anchor your child will come to—not because you were always right, but because you were always there.

BONUS:
Frequently Asked Questions

The "perfect parent" formula doesn't exist. The parent-child relationship is a complex one that comes with questions, doubts, and many messy moments.

Below are some of the most common questions I hear from parents during coaching sessions who are striving to stay connected, calm, and clear while navigating the complexities of raising their child. Let's walk through them together.

1. What if yelling has become the go-to way to express my feelings to my child? Is it too late to repair?

Absolutely not. Yelling may stem from how you were taught to express emotions or from not learning effective emotional expression. It often becomes an automatic reaction. However, it's never too late to change how you manage your anger. As we have covered in Chapter 2, repairing after such incidents is crucial and highly powerful.

If you yell or lose your cool, reconnecting is the key. Be honest and say, "I'm sorry I yelled. That must have been frightening. I wish I had handled it differently." Reconnecting doesn't excuse unwanted behavior, but it does demonstrate accountability. When your child witnesses you taking responsibility, it fosters a sense of respect.

However, be mindful of avoiding a cycle of yelling and apologizing without making any changes. Strive to develop healthier ways of managing emotions and improve consistent communication.

2. How do I stay calm when my child keeps pushing my buttons?

When your child pushes your buttons consciously, avoid reacting immediately. It might not be easy, but it's possible. Take a moment to pause. If necessary, step away briefly. Utilize grounding strategies from Chapter 4: Feel your feet firmly on the ground, take three deep, slow breaths, or remind yourself, "This is challenging, but I can manage it."

Staying calm isn't about suppressing emotion; it's about maintaining the steadiness to lead effectively.

3. My child yells at me. Should there be a consequence?

When your child yells, it can be difficult. Remember to approach the situation with empathy. Recognize that their behavior is communicating underlying emotions. Consider what might be causing their distress—are they hungry, tired, or feeling overwhelmed?

In the moment, prioritize calming the situation rather than reacting with anger. Offer a supportive presence by showing understanding and patience. Once your child has calmed down, gently set a boundary: "I want to hear you, and I'll listen when you can use a calm voice."

This approach not only respects your child's feelings but also teaches them healthier ways to express themselves. When both of you are in a calmer state, discuss the incident. Ask, "What were you feeling? How can we handle this better next time?" This encourages emotional growth without resorting to fear of punishment and fosters a more trusting and respectful relationship.

4. How can I set boundaries without being mean?

Boundaries are a form of love. They give your child something to push against, something safe to hold onto. Being firm doesn't mean being cold. You can say, "I won't let you hit," while staying close, calm, and kind. Think of boundaries as a lighthouse in a storm—they don't chase the boat, but they offer steady guidance.

It's important for you and your partner to be aligned on core values and establish consistent boundaries, such as no hitting, no lies, and being kind. Consistency is the key. For smaller matters, allow flexibility. By focusing on what truly matters and routinely explaining the reasons behind boundaries, children learn to expect and respect them.

5. I feel like I'm the only one doing the emotional work. What should I do?

Feeling like you're the only one carrying the emotional load can be challenging and isolating. It's a struggle many parents face. Open and honest communication with your partner is key. Remember, you both come from unique upbringings, so finding common ground in parenting is essential.

Invite your partner into the conversation positively and without blame. You might say, "Can we chat about our goals for parenting? I feel like we might not be on the same page." Posing questions like these in a non-confrontational way fosters teamwork in your parenting.

6. What if my child doesn't respond after I approach them calmly?

Not every child will immediately soften when you stay calm. Some may need more time, or a different form of regulation like movement, deep pressure, or quiet space.

If your encouragement for them to be calm doesn't work right away, try implementing co-regulation strategies: Stay nearby, stay grounded, and say, "I'm right here. You're safe." You're planting seeds, and even if you don't see an immediate shift, your presence is helping their nervous system settle.

7. How do I teach emotional regulation without giving in?

Validating feelings doesn't mean removing boundaries. You can (and should!) acknowledge your child's feelings.

Try: "You're really upset, but you can't have that toy," and hold the boundary that you've set in place in the past. That's the essence of emotion coaching: Welcoming emotion while maintaining rules. When kids feel seen and contained, they learn that big feelings are safe to express, but not in harmful ways.

8. What if I lose my temper often? Am I damaging my child?

Frequent yelling can impact your child negatively, affecting their emotional and social development. It might cause them to feel unsafe or anxious, and they may learn to express their own emotions by yelling back in return. It's essential to ensure your child isn't a victim of your anger.

Acknowledging the impact that you have on your child is the first step towards change. Reflect on what's fueling your anger—stress, exhaustion, or deeper emotional issues. Understanding these triggers helps you manage your emotional responses more effectively.

It's important to seek support if you can't make these changes on your own, whether through therapy, coaching, or by clearly communicating your needs to someone who can help you. These actions can help you develop healthier ways of managing emotions and create a nurturing environment for your child.

With conscious effort and awareness, you can model positive emotional regulation for your child, fostering a safe and loving relationship.

9. Why does it feel like I'm the only one my child shows unwanted behavior with?

Children often act in front of those they feel most comfortable with, much like they might behave with their grandparents, who meet all their needs. It's a sign of trust when your child feels at ease with you, but it's essential to establish boundaries around unwanted behavior. Children need guidance and teaching as well as love and support.

If you feel hurt by your child's behavior towards you, take a moment to evaluate your boundaries. Ensure you're maintaining them consistently. As children grow, it becomes more challenging to manage misbehavior, so establishing clear boundaries early is key.

10. How do I know if I'm doing this right?

If you're reading this book, you're already on the right path. You care, you're present, and you're committed to growth. These are crucial steps in parenting. Focusing on understanding your child's perspective can significantly reduce moments of frustration.

Keep striving to see the world through their eyes. This approach not only strengthens your connection but also enriches your parenting experience. Trust in your efforts and continue to learn and adapt—you're doing wonderfully.

REFERENCE AND FURTHER READING

- Champion Your Parenting. (2023). *How to Respond, Not React to My Kids.*
  https://www.championyourparenting.com/how-to-respond-not-react-to-my-kids/
- Pediatric Care Group. (2021). *Responding vs. Reacting.*
  https://pcgkids.com/2021/11/10/responding-vs-reacting-2/
- Harvard Health Publishing. (2018). *Understanding the Stress Response.*
  https://www.health.harvard.edu/mind-and-mood/understanding-the-stress-response
- Gottman Institute. (2020). *The Four Parenting Styles and Emotion Coaching.*
  https://www.gottman.com/blog/the-four-parenting-styles/
- Gottman Institute. (2021). *Positive Parenting: Accept the Feelings, Limit the Actions.*
  https://www.gottman.com/blog/positive-parenting-accept-feelings-limit-actions/
- Lovevery. (2022). *Dr. Becky on the Importance of Empathy.*
  https://blog.lovevery.com/podcast/dr-becky-on-the-importance-of-empathy/
- NC State Extension. (2024). *Building Relationships with Your Child by Active Listening.*
  https://randolph.ces.ncsu.edu/2024/05/building-relationships-with-your-child-by-active-listening/
- Iowa State University. (2023). *Active Listening.*
  https://iastate.pressbooks.pub/parentingfamilydiversity/chapter/active-listening/

- American Psychological Association. (2021). *Parental Burnout Is Real.*
  https://www.apa.org/monitor/2021/10/cover-parental-burnout
- Australian Psychological Society. (2023). *Feeling Drained by Parenting Choices? Tips to Lighten the Load.*
  https://psychology.org.au/about-us/news-and-media/aps-in-the-media/2023/feeling-drained-by-parenting-choices-tips-to-light
- Good Inside. (2023). *Emotional Regulation in Children.*
  https://www.goodinside.com/blog/emotional-regulation-in-children/
- Sim, J. (2018). *5Rs: No-Yelling Formula for Consequences. Work Life Kids.*
  https://www.worklifekids.com/blog/2018/12/2/5rs-no-yelling-formula-for-consequences
- Positive Parenting Solutions. (n.d.). *Effective Consequences for Misbehavior.*
  https://www.positiveparentingsolutions.com/effective-consequences-for-misbehavior/
- Gottman Institute. (n.d.). *An Introduction to Emotion Coaching.*
  https://www.gottman.com/blog/an-introduction-to-emotion-coaching/
- Siegel, D. J. (n.d.). *Whole-Brain Child Handouts.*
  https://drdansiegel.com/whole-brain-child-handouts/
- Brackett, M. A. (n.d.). *Yale Center for Emotional Intelligence.*
  https://marcbrackett.com/yale-center-for-emotional-intelligence/
- C.S. Mott Children's Hospital. (2024). *The Emotion 63% of Parents Aren't Sure They Know How To Help Their Kids With.*
  https://www.parents.com/emotion-parents-cant-help-their-kids-with-8748317
- Child Mind Institute. (n.d.). *Angry Kids: Dealing With Explosive Behavior.*
  https://childmind.org/article/angry-kids-dealing-with-explosive-behavior/
- Harvard University. (2023). *The Secret Ingredient to Stronger Parent-Child Relationships.*

- https://mcc.gse.harvard.edu/whats-new/secret-ingredient-parent-child-relationships
- Frontiers in Psychology. (2024). *The Central Role of Mindful Parenting.* https://www.frontiersin.org/articles/10.3389/fpsyg.2024.1420588/full
- American Psychological Association. (2023). *How to Help Kids Understand and Manage Their Emotions.* https://www.apa.org/topics/parenting/emotion-regulation
- Coming Home Therapy. (n.d.). *Being the Parent You Want to Be.* https://cominghometherapy.ca/being-the-parent-you-want-to-be/
- Lori, J. (2023). *How to Tell If You Are Repeating an Inherited Parenting Pattern.* https://medium.com/@lori_86546/how-to-tell-if-you-are-repeating-an-inherited-a-parenting-pattern-cccf503eea4f
- CW Live Your Truth. (2022). *Stop Repeating Your Parents' Dysfunctional Patterns.* https://cw.liveyourtruth.com/stop-repeating-your-parents-dysfunctional-patterns/
- This Time of Mine. (2022). *Getting Kids to Listen: 10 Alternatives to Yelling.* https://thistimeofmine.com/10-powerful-alternatives-to-yelling/
- Michigan Alliance for Families. (n.d.). *Behavior is Communication.* https://www.michiganallianceforfamilies.org/behavior-is-communication/
- Shalders, L. (2015). *How to Peacefully Teach and Set Clear Limits, Boundaries, and Consequences with Your Child.* https://www.louiseshalders.com.au/articles/2015/10/14/how-to-peacefully-teach-and-set-clear-limits-boundaries-and-consequences-with-your-child
- Parenting Place. (2023). *How to Set Boundaries That Actually Work.* https://parentingplace.nz/resources/how-to-set-boundaries-that-actually-work/

www.ingramcontent.com/pod-product-compliance
Lightning Source LLC
Chambersburg PA
CBHW020247010526
44107CB00002B/143